# *Beyond Basic*
# CROCHETING

# *Beyond Basic* CROCHETING

## Techniques and Projects to Expand Your Skills

Sharon Hernes Silverman

Additional designs by
Kristin Omdahl
Annie Modesitt

Photographs by
Alan Wycheck

Illustrations by
David Bienkowski

STACKPOLE
BOOKS

Copyright © 2007 by Stackpole Books

Published by
STACKPOLE BOOKS
5067 Ritter Road
Mechanicsburg, PA 17055
www.stackpolebooks.com

Printed in China

10  9  8  7  6  5  4  3  2  1

FIRST EDITION

*Photographs by Alan Wycheck*
*Illustrations by David Bienkowski*
*Cover design by Tracy Patterson*

Beaded wrap and motif sweater designs © Kristin Omdahl.
Socks and wire necklace designs © Annie Modesitt. Used
with permission of the designers. All other patterns © Sharon
Hernes Silverman.

Crocheting Abbreviations Master List, Standard Body Mea-
surements/Sizing, and Standard Yarn Weight System charts
used courtesy of the Craft Yarn Council of America (CYCA),
*www.yarnstandards.com.*

**Library of Congress Cataloging-in-Publication Data**

Silverman, Sharon Hernes.
  Beyond basic crocheting : techniques and projects to expand
your skills / Sharon Hernes Silverman ; additional designs by
Kristin Omdahl, Annie Modesitt ; photographs by Alan
Wycheck ; illustrations by David Bienkowski. — 1st ed.
      p. cm.
  ISBN-13: 978-0-8117-3392-2 (alk. paper)
  ISBN-10: 0-8117-3392-0 (alk. paper)
  1. Crocheting—Patterns. I. Omdahl, Kristin. II. Modesitt,
Annie. III. Title.

TT820.S5263 2007
746.43'4041—dc22
                                              2007003172

# Contents

# Acknowledgments

Writing *Beyond Basic Crocheting* was a joy for me, thanks in large part to the encouragement and support I received from many people.

Kristin Omdahl (*www.styledbykristin.com*) and Annie Modesitt (*www.anniemodesitt.com*) provided beautiful, creative designs and the detailed instructions to go with them. Photographer Alan Wycheck (*www.alanwycheck photo.com*) diligently documented every step in every project and took amazing pictures of the finished items. David Bienkowski's illustrations depict crocheted stitches so clearly that it would be impossible not to understand how to execute them. His art extends far beyond technical illustrations; view David's paintings on his website (*www.art-db.com*).

Terri McClure demonstrated the crocheting techniques for the camera with skill, stamina, and good humor. Elizabeth Hofmann modeled finished projects with style and grace. Thanks also to Autumn Wycheck for modeling the girl's jumper, and to her mom, Cindy, and her doggie Boo for keeping her company.

Mark Allison, editor, and Judith M. Schnell, publisher and vice president of Stackpole Books, spoiled me completely with their enthusiasm. Other members of the Stackpole team—Amy D. Lerner, Tracy Patterson, Caroline Stover, Amy Wagner, Donna Pope, and Ken Krawchuk—also brought their editorial, design, marketing, and publishing expertise to this project, for which they have my eternal gratitude.

With the support of Mark and Judith, I was able to travel to Los Angeles to crochet on three episodes of *Uncommon Threads*, produced by the Home and Garden Television (HGTV) network in association with the Do-It-Yourself (DIY) network. My crocheting companions on this wonderful adventure were Julianne Eisele and Naomi Ramos. These ladies were stars in my book long before their television debut. Thanks are due to Assistant Producers Lorelei Plotczyk and Joy Wingard, to host Alison Whitlock, and to the rest of the *Uncommon Threads* staff.

JoAnne Turcotte of Plymouth Yarn Company supplied the yarn used in the beaded wrap and the motif cardigan; Jean Guirguis of Lion Brand Yarn provided the bunny rabbit yarn. Thanks to Mary Colucci, executive director of the Craft Yarn Council of America, for permission to reprint charts of yarn industry standards.

I am grateful to Anita Closic, owner of A Garden of Yarn in Chadds Ford, Pennsylvania (*www.agardenof yarn.com*), for inviting me to teach classes at her friendly, well-stocked shop.

A big thank-you to the students who attended my classes or learned to crochet from *Basic Crocheting*. I am delighted that you are enjoying the craft. Your requests for more projects motivated me to put together the current volume.

Much appreciation to my parents, Babe and Seymour Hernes, and to other family members and friends who always cheer me on, not just through my writing projects, but through life in general. Special mention goes to Janet Napoli, my forever friend, whose email presence has been wonderfully reassuring during many a late night of work.

Most of all, love and thanks to my husband, Alan Silverman, and our sons, Jason and Steven.

# Introduction

*Beyond Basic Crocheting* is designed for people who are comfortable with basic crochet stitches and who are eager to try more challenging projects and learn new techniques. What makes the book unique is its focus on crystal clear instructions, supplemented by a large number of photographs and illustrations. No steps are skipped; no assumptions are made about what you already know. Think of *Beyond Basic Crocheting* as an experienced friend sitting nearby to answer your questions and guide you to success.

The first part of the book presents a brief review of fundamental stitches, techniques, and materials, and introduces some tools and materials that were not used in *Basic Crocheting*. The second part of the book includes patterns for nine projects. Skill workshops focus on specific techniques relevant to each item. Designs were selected for their stylishness and variety.

If you are new to crocheting, please use *Basic Crocheting* as your introduction and return to this book when you are comfortable with the essentials.

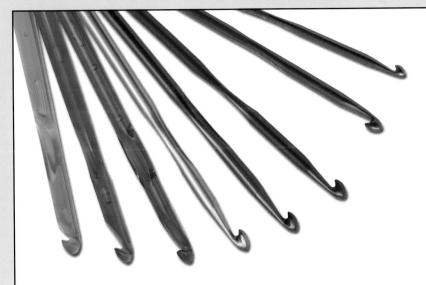

# Part I

## Materials and Basic Skills Review

## Yarn

### COLOR
Commercially manufactured yarn is dyed in batches, or lots, which can have slight variations. To avoid color discrepancies, purchase enough yarn to complete your project. Check the codes on the labels to make sure the yarn is from one dye lot.

### WEIGHT
Yarn comes in weight from super fine to super bulky. To make the finished project look like the designer intended, use the recommended weight. If you want to substitute one yarn for another, make sure it is in the same weight category.

**The CYCA's six yarn weight categories
(see also the standard yarn weight system appendix):
Super Fine, Fine, Light, Medium, Bulky, Super Bulky**

### Wire
Yarn isn't the only material you can crochet. This book introduces you to the technique of crocheting with wire. Wire comes in a variety of colors and finishes. The thickness of the wire is expressed in its gauge. The lower the number, the thicker it is. Gauge from 28 to 32 is ideal for crocheting.

When you are working with wire, pliers and a wire cutter come in handy.

## Hooks

The crochet hook is your basic tool.

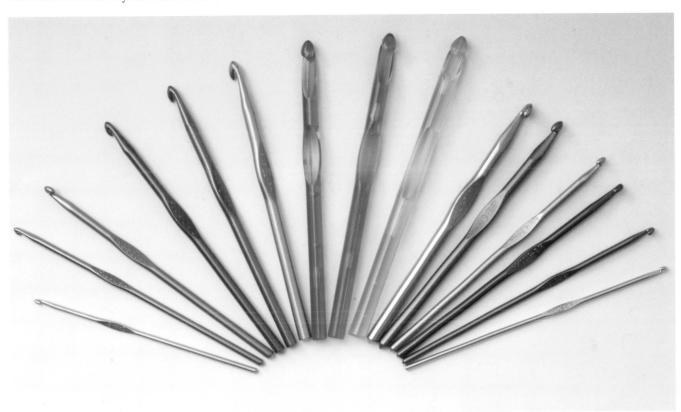

In addition to the standard hooks, there are specialty hooks. An afghan hook, or Tunisian hook, is a long hook with a stopper on the end. The double-ended hook is similar to the afghan hook, but it has a hook on each end. These long hooks are useful for Tunisian crochet projects, in which the loops for each row remain on the hook and are then worked off.

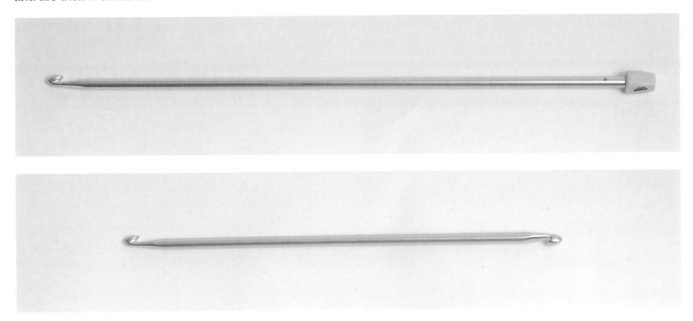

## Beads

Incorporating beads into crocheted work brings an added level of sophistication. When choosing beads, take their weight, hole size, and shape into account.

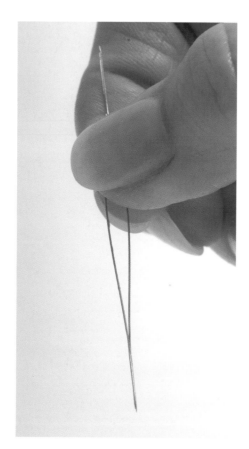

A big-eye beading needle is helpful for prestringing beads onto yarn.

## Handbag Handles

To dress up a finished handbag, choose from among the wide variety of prefabricated handles available.

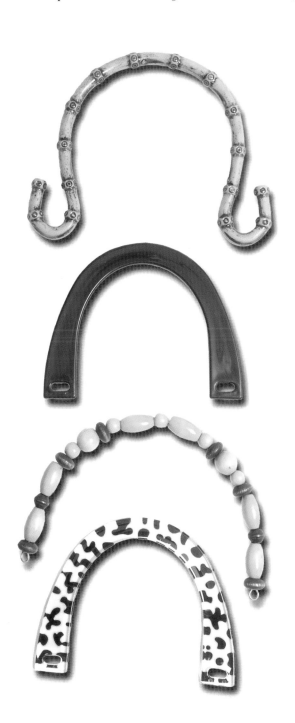

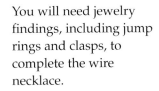

You will need jewelry findings, including jump rings and clasps, to complete the wire necklace.

## Other Handy Tools

- scissors or yarn cutter
- tape measure
- tapestry needles
- pins
- hook/stitch gauge
- row counters
- steam iron or steamer
- safety pins.

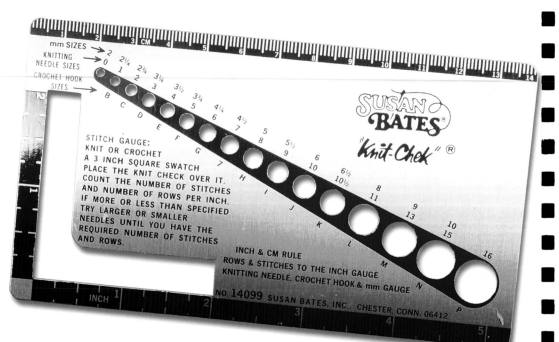

## BASIC SKILLS REVIEW

### Holding the Hook

Hold the hook like a pencil . . .

. . . or a knife.

### Making a Slip Knot

A slip knot attaches the yarn to the hook.

**1.** Make a pretzel shape of your yarn. Put the hook over one circle and pick up the yarn underneath.

**2.** Pull ends apart to tighten.

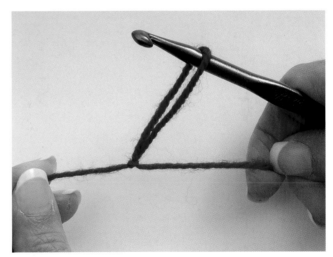

## Chain Stitch

**1.** Wrap the yarn over the hook from back to front. Pull through.

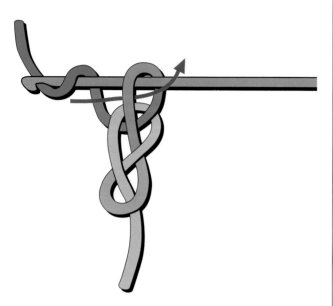

Most items start with a row of chain stitches. If you find that your chains are tighter than your other stitches, use a bigger hook for the chains. Switch back to a smaller hook to continue.

## Slip Stitch

**1.** Insert hook into work.

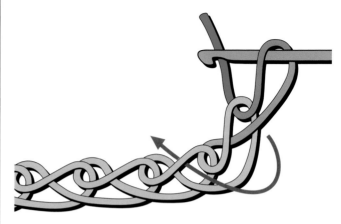

**2.** Wrap yarn over and pull through both loops.

The low-profile slip stitch is used to join the ends when crocheting in the round, and to move the hook over without adding height to the work.

## Single Crochet

**1.** Insert hook into work (usually this will be in the second stitch from the hook for the first stitch after the foundation chain).

**2.** Wrap yarn over and pull through to front.

**3.** Wrap yarn over and pull through both loops.

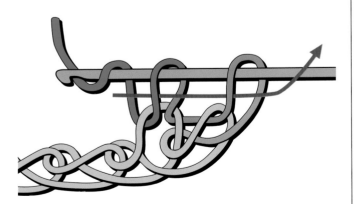

## Half Double Crochet

**1.** Wrap the yarn over the hook. Insert into work (usually this will be in the third stitch from the hook for the first stitch after the foundation chain).

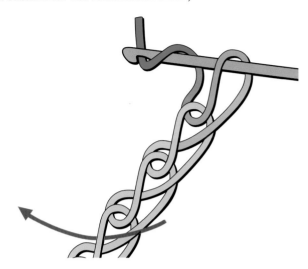

**2.** Wrap yarn over and pull through to front.

**3.** Wrap yarn over again and pull through all 3 loops.

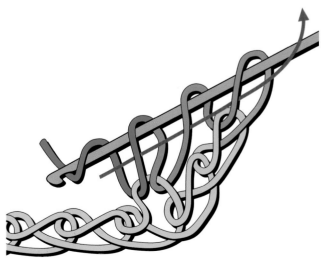

## Double Crochet

**1.** Wrap the yarn over the hook. Insert into work (usually this will be in the fourth chain from the hook for the first stitch after the foundation chain).

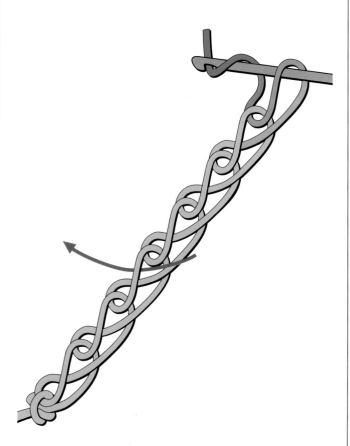

**2.** Wrap yarn over and pull through to front.

**3.** Wrap yarn over and pull through 2 loops.

**4.** Wrap yarn over and pull through remaining 2 loops.

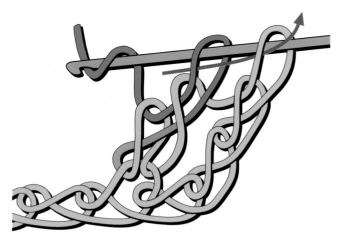

## Working in Rows

The important thing about working in rows is to keep the number of stitches consistent. This can be tricky at the beginning and end of a row. Typically, you will make several chain stitches at the beginning of a row to equal the height of the stitches that will follow.

After you make your foundation chains, you will be instructed to work your first stitch a specified number of chains away from the loop on the hook. This allows the last few chains—the number varies depending on the type of stitch—to stand up straight and act as the first stitch in the row.

The same principle holds on subsequent rows. Chain stitches serve as placeholders for the first stitch. Here are guidelines for how many turning chains to make for standard stitches. If you find that the suggested number of chains makes your stitch too short or too tall, alter it so it more closely matches the subsequent stitches.

| | |
|---|---|
| Single crochet | 1 |
| Half double crochet | 2 |
| Double crochet | 3 |

**1.** For practice, work a double crochet row. After the foundation chains, work your first stitch into the fourth chain from the hook. At the end of the row, chain stitch 3.

**2.** After you make the turning chains, do not insert the hook at their base. Because those chains count as a stitch, this would mean you would have two stitches where you should only have one, inadvertently increasing the number of stitches. If you notice that your work is getting wider, check to make sure you are not working a stitch at the base of the turning chain. Skip the base of the turning chains unless you are instructed otherwise.

**3.** At the far end of the row, work your last stitch into the topmost chain from the previous row; otherwise you will inadvertently decrease the number of stitches. If your work starts getting narrower, check to make sure you are working a stitch in this spot.

It does not matter whether you turn your work clockwise or counterclockwise, but it will look neater if you are consistent.

## Joining a New Yarn

You will need to join a new yarn when you finish a ball or when you want to change colors. If possible, do this in the last 2 stitches of a row.

**1.** Work your stitch up to the next-to-last step. In other words, do not put the yarn over and pull through to complete the stitch. Let the old yarn hang to the back of the work.

**2.** Put the new yarn over the hook and pull through to complete the stitch.

**3.** Continue working with the new yarn, making sure you are using the working end of the yarn and not the short tail.

Notice that all parts of the first complete stitch with the new color are in that color, and no parts of the previous stitch are. Adding new yarn at the top of the previous stitch—as the last step in completing that stitch—has this happy result.

## Fastening Off

Simply cut the yarn a few inches from the hook, wrap yarn over, and pull through so the tail comes through also. Pull gently to tighten. Don't cut the yarn too short; it is easier to weave it in later if it is a few inches long.

## Weaving in Ends

Use a small crochet hook or a tapestry needle to weave the ends through stitches on the wrong side of your work, and then clip the ends close.

**Tip:** You can hold short ends snugly next to the work as you go along, crocheting subsequent stitches around them. This reduces the need to weave ends in later.

## Measuring Gauge

Gauge is the number of stitches (or pattern repeats) and rows to a given measurement. Everyone crochets differently, so even if 2 people are using the same yarn, stitches, and hook, their gauges can vary.

For your work to be the right size, match the recommended gauge as closely as possible.

**1.** Work a swatch about 6 inches square using the hook, yarn, and stitches specified in the pattern.

**Tip:** Block your gauge swatch before measuring gauge to make certain that your finished item will be the desired size after it is blocked.

**2.** Using your gauge measurer or a rigid tape measure (not a fabric one), count the number of stitches and the number of rows you made. Compare this to the recommended gauge.

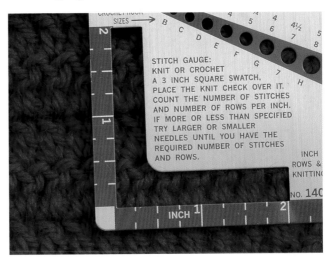

If you have more stitches or rows than you are supposed to, your gauge is too tight. Try again with a larger hook. If you have fewer rows or stitches than you are supposed to, your gauge is too loose. Try a smaller hook.

Sometimes your gauge is not equal horizontally and vertically. It is more important to match the number of stitches than the number of rows.

## Blocking

Steam blocking smoothes stitches, shapes a garment, squares the corners, flattens ends, and gives a professional finish.

**1.** Lay the item facedown on a padded surface like a towel or an ironing board cover. Using stainless steel pins, pin pieces in place, shaping them into the form they should be.

**2.** If you have a steam iron, hover just above the crocheted pieces; the steam will set the stitches. Do not let the weight of the iron press the stitches, because it will flatten them. Another alternative is to place a damp cloth on top of the items. Gently place a warm iron down on the cloth, then lift it and move it to another part of the item. Do not slide the iron around.

**3.** Let the pieces cool and dry before unpinning. The fabric will be nice and soft.

Block your gauge swatch to make sure it matches the recommended gauge. If it changes the gauge, switch to a different size hook, make another swatch, and block it. This will ensure that your finished, blocked item is the right size.

## Reading a Pattern

Crocheting uses standard abbreviations. A master list of abbreviations, as prepared by the Craft Yarn Council of America, is on the following page. Not all of the abbreviations are used in this book, but it is good to become familiar with them as you move on to other projects.

Parentheses ( ) or brackets [ ] are often used to enclose a sequence of instructions meant to be repeated. After the closing parenthesis or bracket, you'll be told how many times to repeat the instructions.

For example, "[2 dc in next dc, 1 ch] twice" means to do 2 double crochet stitches in the next double crochet (from the row below), 1 chain stitch, 2 double crochet stitches in the next double crochet, 1 chain stitch.

Sometimes parentheses are just for explanatory information. For example, "(the second of the 3 double crochet stitches in the corner)" tells you the position of the stitch.

An asterisk * means to work the instructions following it as many more times as indicated. For example, if the instructions say, "Repeat from * to end of row," you would keep doing the stitch or pattern following the asterisk until you get to the end. Sometimes an asterisk is also used to mark the end of the sequence. If the instructions say, "Repeat from * to * 3 more times," you would execute the instructions between the asterisks and then do that again 3 additional times.

## Healthy Crocheting

Crocheting is not strenuous, but it is physical and uses repetitive motions. To avoid strain and injury, it is important to work comfortably and not to do too much at one time, especially at first. Here are some guidelines for healthy crocheting:

- Use a chair with good back support.
- Don't try to hold a heavy project, like a blanket, as it gets unwieldy. Work at a surface where you can lay the project down.
- Use adequate lighting.
- Use reading glasses or a magnifier on a stand if necessary.
- Take a break every 20 to 30 minutes to walk around, stretch your neck, arms, and legs, and give your eyes a rest.
- If you ever feel pain or discomfort while crocheting, STOP.

## Crocheting Abbreviations Master List

Following is a list of crochet abbreviations used in patterns by yarn industry designers and publishers. The most commonly used abbreviations are highlighted. In addition, designers and publishers may use special abbreviations in a pattern, which you might not find on this list. Generally, a definition of special abbreviations is given at the beginning of a book or pattern.

| Abbreviation | Description |
|---|---|
| [ ] | work instructions within brackets as many times as directed |
| ( ) | work instructions within parentheses as many times as directed |
| * | repeat the instructions following the single asterisk as directed |
| * * | repeat instructions between asterisks as many times as directed or repeat from a given set of instructions |
| " | inch(es) |
| alt | alternate |
| **approx** | approximately |
| **beg** | begin/beginning |
| **bet** | between |
| **BL** | back loop(s) |
| bo | bobble |
| **BP** | back post |
| **BPdc** | back post double crochet |
| BPsc | back post single crochet |
| BPtr | back post treble crochet |
| CA | color A |
| CB | color B |
| **CC** | contrasting color |
| **ch** | chain stitch |
| **ch-** | refers to chain or space previously made: e.g., ch-1 space |
| **ch-sp** | chain space |
| CL | cluster |
| cm | centimeter(s) |
| **cont** | continue |
| **dc** | double crochet |
| **dc2tog** | double crochet 2 stitches together |
| **dec** | decrease/decreases/decreasing |
| dtr | double treble |
| **FL** | front loop(s) |
| **foll** | follow/follows/following |
| **FP** | front post |

| Abbreviation | Description |
|---|---|
| **FPdc** | front post double crochet |
| **FPsc** | front post single crochet |
| **FPtr** | front post treble crochet |
| **g** | gram |
| **hdc** | half double crochet |
| **inc** | increase/increases/increasing |
| **lp(s)** | loops |
| m | meter(s) |
| **MC** | main color |
| **mm** | millimeter(s) |
| **oz** | ounce(s) |
| p | picot |
| **pat(s)** or **patt** | pattern(s) |
| pc | popcorn |
| pm | place marker |
| prev | previous |
| **rem** | remain/remaining |
| **rep** | repeat(s) |
| **rnd(s)** | round(s) |
| **RS** | right side |
| **sc** | single crochet |
| **sc2tog** | single crochet 2 stitches together |
| **sk** | skip |
| **Sl st** | slip sitich |
| **sp(s)** | space(s) |
| **st(s)** | stitch(es) |
| tch or t-ch | turning chain |
| tbl | through back loop |
| **tog** | together |
| **tr** | treble crochet |
| trtr | triple treble crochet |
| **WS** | wrong side |
| **yd(s)** | yard(s) |
| **yo** | yarn over |
| yoh | yarn over hook |

# Part II

## Projects

# 1
# Beaded Wrap

This gorgeous garment has "Wow!" written all over it. Luscious baby alpaca yarn, glistening beads, and a variety of stitches envelop the wearer in style. The way the beaded picots are framed in little archways gives this wrap an interesting architectural look.

**Finished size:** 27 inches x 68 inches

## Materials:

Plymouth Yarn Baby Alpaca D.K.
   (100 percent superfine baby alpaca, 50
   grams/1.8 ounces, 125 yards/114 meters)

14 balls color 1720

Hook: H/5 mm or size needed to
   obtain gauge

Big-eye beading needle

1,800 size 6 hexagonal Matsuno beads,
   color 1 (clear/silver)

## Stitches and abbreviations:

Chain stitch (ch)

Half double crochet (hdc)

Double crochet together (dc tog)

Skip (sk)

Slip stitch (sl st)

Stitch (st)

Treble crochet (tr); this is
   also known as triple
   crochet

Yo (yarn over)

1-bead picot

3-bead picot

**Note:** To work 2 dc tog, yo and insert
hook into next stitch. Pull up loop, yo, and
pull through 2 loops. Stop there: do not
complete the stitch. Yo again, insert hook
into the next stitch, and pull up the loop.
Yo and pull through 2 loops; yo and pull
through all 3 remaining loops.

   To work a tr, yo twice, insert hook into
stitch, pull up loop (4 loops on hook). Yo,
pull through 2 loops (3 loops remain on
hook). Yo and pull through 2 loops (2 loops
remain on hook). Yo and pull through last
2 loops.

   (See Skill Workshops for instructions for
1-bead picot and 3-bead picot.)

## Gauge:

3 stitches in pattern/1 inch; 2 rows in
   pattern/ 1 inch (after blocking). Make a
   swatch and block it before checking
   your gauge. Gauge is somewhat
   forgiving in this one-size project, but
   you don't want to be too far off.

**Tip:** Check with your source to find out how many beads
come in a tube; the tubes used for this project contained
approximately 280 beads/tube. Always buy an extra tube
so you don't run out of beads.

## Beaded Wrap

Prestring beads. (See tip below to figure out how many to string at a time.) Attach yarn to hook with slip knot. Ch 92.

**Row 1 (wrong side):** Work 1 sc into second ch from hook, 1 sc into next ch. *Ch 1, slip 1 bead and ch 3, sl stitch into fourth ch from hook just below bead (1-bead picot made), 1 sc into each of the next 3 ch; repeat from * across, ending with 2 sc instead of 3 sc. Turn.

**Row 2 (right side):** Ch 5 (counts as 1 dc and ch 2), skip over beaded picot to sc centered between 2 picots, 1 dc into that sc, *ch 2, skip 2 sc, 1 dc into next sc; repeat from * to end. Turn.

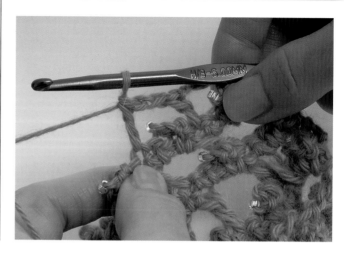

**Tip:** Beads are prestrung and pulled into place as the pattern specifies. The remainder of the prestrung beads have to be moved out of the way as you go along. How many beads to string is a matter of personal preference. Some crocheters like to string just a few rows of beads before starting. In this project there are 30 beads on every other row; stringing 90 beads plus a few extra, just in case, will get you through 6 rows. When you run out of beads, you have to cut the yarn, prestring beads onto the next segment of yarn, rejoin the yarn, and resume crocheting. Try to do this at the end of a row. (Alternatively, if you don't have that much yarn left, you can unroll the ball and string the beads from the other end.)

Be careful to slide the beads gently so they do not damage the yarn. Move just a few at a time, starting with the ones that are farthest from your hook.

Beads are slid into place and crocheted on wrong side rows, but they will show on the right side.

**Tip:** The double crochets are placed in the center of the 3 single crochets from the previous row, framing the picots between the double crochets.

**Row 3:** Ch 1, sc into first dc (at the base of the turning ch), *into next ch 2 sp work (sc, 1-bead picot, sc), sc into next dc; repeat from * to end, placing last sc into third ch of ch 5 from previous row.

**Rows 4–51:** Repeat rows 2 and 3 twenty-four more times. Fasten off.

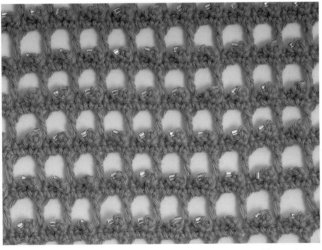

Turn the completed work around. You will work again into the starting chain. The next part of the wrap you'll make is the unbeaded center, followed by beading that matches the section you just completed. The rows are counted starting again at row 1. You do not need to string any beads until completing row 25, so do not prestring any now.

## UNBEADED CENTER

**Row 1:** Join to corner of starting ch with sl st. Ch 3 (counts as first dc), dc in next ch, (ch 1, sk 1 ch below, dc 2 tog in next ch) across. Turn.

**Row 2:** Ch 3, dc (ch 1, skip 1 st below, dc 2 tog in next st) across. Turn. Total 46 clusters of 2 dc including the initial ch 3 and dc, which counts as a dc cluster.

**Rows 3–25:** Repeat row 2.

Now you will create the other beaded end of the wrap. String 90 beads. (If you are near the end of the yarn ball, string the beads from the far end. If not, cut the yarn, string the beads, and reattach the yarn with a sl st.)

**Tip:** Make sure that the beads on this end of the wrap are going to show on the same side as the other beaded end. In other words, you should work them on wrong-side rows so they show on the right side. If necessary, repeat row 2 once more to make sure the beads show through properly.

**Row 26:** Ch 1, sc into first dc, *sc into next ch sp, 1-bead picot, sc into next dc and next ch sp, sc into next dc, 1 bead picot, sc into next ch sp and next dc, repeat from * 14 times, ending with 1 sc. Total 30 picots.

**Row 27:** Ch 5 (counts as 1 dc and ch 2), skip over beaded picot to sc centered between 2 picots, 1 dc into that sc, *ch 2, skip 2 sc, 1 dc into next sc; repeat from * to end. Turn.

**Tip:** As in the first beaded section, the double crochets are placed in the center of the 3 single crochets from the previous row, framing the picots between the double crochets.

**Row 28:** Ch 1, sc into first dc (at the base of the turning ch), *into next ch 2 sp work (sc, 1-bead picot, sc), sc into next dc; repeat from * to end, placing last sc into third ch of ch 5 from previous row.

**Rows 29–76:** Repeat rows 2 and 3 twenty-four more times, ending with a row of double crochet frames. Fasten off.

## EDGING

With right-side facing, start on a short side, with the corner first. Attach yarn in corner with sl st.

**Tip:** The edging has 3 rounds. The first round works sc stitches evenly around the wrap. The second round sets up an openwork foundation. The third round puts scallops with 3-bead picots in place. You will not turn the wrap as you move from 1 round to the next.

**Round 1:** Work 3 sc into corner, *(2 sc into ch 2 sp, sc into dc) across to next corner, 3 sc into corner. Along edge of rows, work (2 sc into ends of all dc rows and 1 sc into ends of all sc rows) across to next corner, 3 sc into corner; repeat from * once more. Sl st into first sc to join. Do not turn.

**Round 2:** Sl st into center sc of corner. Ch 11 (counts as dc and ch 8), dc into same space to make a big loop, ch 8. [*Skip 5 sts, dc into next st, ch 8*, repeat from * to * across to next corner, work (dc, ch 8, dc) into corner stitch.] Repeat instructions in [ ] twice more, then from * to * once more. Sl st into third ch at beginning of round. Do not turn.

**Tip:** Work over any loose ends as you go along to weave them in.

**Round 3:** Sl st into first ch 8 space. [Sc, hdc, dc, 3 tr, (ch 1, slip 3 beads, ch 2, sl st into third ch from hook, just below the beads, to complete 3-bead picot), 2 tr, dc, hdc, sc]. Repeat instructions in [ ] in each ch 8 space around. Sl st into first sc to join. Fasten off.

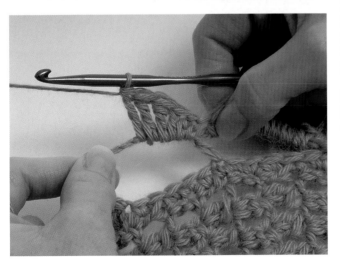

**Tip:** The pattern in round 3 uses stitches of increasing then decreasing heights to form a scallop shape. A 3-bead picot is worked on top of the third treble crochet stitch, the center of the 5 trebles that form the apex of the scallop.

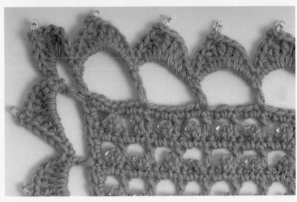

## FINISHING
Weave in loose ends. Steam block.

# SKILL WORKSHOP: PRESTRINGING BEADS

**1.** Put the end of the yarn through the large eye of the beading needle.

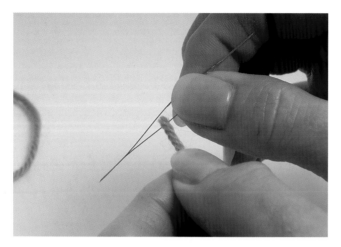

**2.** Use the end of the needle to pick up several beads.

**Tip:** Both ends of the big-eye beading needle are very sharp. Be careful. Rather than holding the beads and trying to manipulate the needle into the hole, pour some beads onto a table or into a shallow dish and pick them up that way. When you are done with the needle, return it to its original packaging so nobody gets poked.

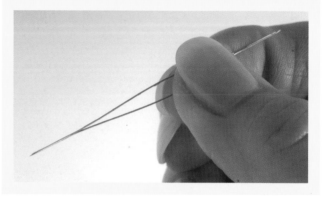

**3.** Slide the beads past the needle onto the yarn.

**4.** Push the beads down the yarn away from the needle. Spread the beads out as you go. You will slide them into position for the picots.

**1.** Work a sc where indicated by the pattern. In this case, it is in the "window" made by the ch of the previous row.

**2.** Ch 1. Slide a bead snugly up to the stitch you just completed.

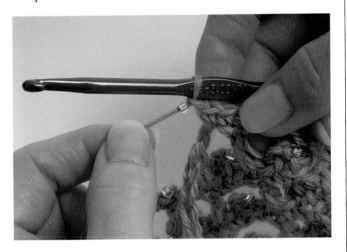

**3.** Ch 1 to secure the bead in place.

**4.** Ch 2 more.

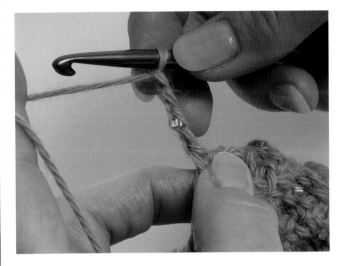

**5.** Find the fourth ch from the hook. It is the one just below the bead.

**6.** Work a sl st into that ch to complete the picot.

**Beaded Wrap**

**1.** There are 5 total treble crochet stitches in each scallop on the outermost row of trim. The 3-bead picot is worked atop the center (third) treble.

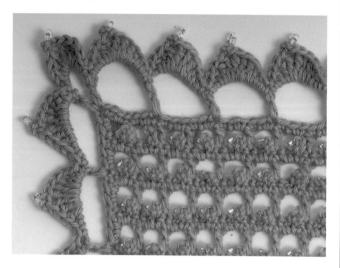

**2.** Ch 1. Slide 3 beads snugly up to the stitch you just completed.

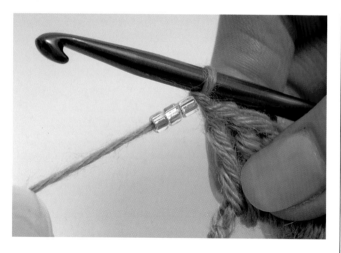

**Tip:** The 3-bead picot is worked in similar fashion to the 1-bead picot. There are 2 differences. First, instead of sliding just 1 bead into place, 3 beads are slid together. Second, only 2 chain stitches are worked after the beads are snugged up to the hook—1 to secure the beads and 1 more—instead of 3.

**3.** Ch 1 to secure the bead in place.

**4.** Ch 1 more.

**5.** Find the third ch from the hook. It is the one just below the beads.

**6.** Work a sl st into that ch to complete the picot. Continue in pattern.

# 2

# Tunisian Crochet Scarf

Tunisian crochet, also known as afghan stitch, combines the best aspects of crocheting and knitting. As you work one direction, loops are left on the hook. When you go the other direction, they are worked off the hook. The front looks like a crocheted piece, while the back resembles a knitted fabric.

Variegated yarn is perfect for Tunisian crochet because the vertical bars contrast with the horizontal stitches behind them. Tunisian's tailored look makes this scarf equally suitable for men and women.

**Finished size:** Approximately 4¹/₂ inches wide x 50 inches long

**Materials:**

Filatura di Crossa 127 Print yarn

2 skeins color 35 (100 percent wool, 50 grams/1³/₄ ounces, 93 yards/85 meters)

Hook: Size K or size needed to obtain gauge

**Gauge:**

7 Tss (Tunisian simple stitch)/2 inches; 6 rows Tss/2 inches. Gauge is not extremely important for this project.

**Stitches and abbreviations:**

Chain stitch (ch)

Single crochet (sc)

Slip stitch (sl st)

Space (sp)

Tunisian simple stitch (Tss)

Yarn over (yo)

**Tip:** Because the scarf is only 4¹/₂ inches wide, you can use a regular K hook. If you have a size K afghan hook—a very long hook with a stopper on one end—or a size K double-ended hook, you could use either one of those.

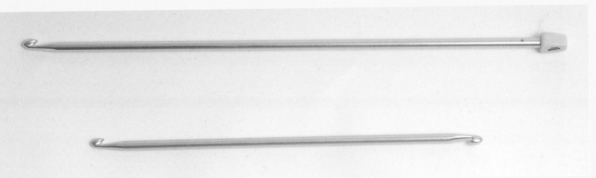

Tunisian fabric is dense. It is important to work fairly loosely. If a K hook gives you tight stitches, switch to a larger size hook.

**Tip:** There are many Tunisian stitches, including Tunisian knit, purl, bobble, basketweave, and cluster. Tunisian simple stitch is an ideal introduction to this back-and-forth technique. A swatch done in Tunisian simple stitch shows the knit-crochet combination vividly: the front looks like crocheted fabric and the back looks like it was knitted in stockinette stitch.

## Tunisian Crochet Scarf

**Foundation row:** Attach yarn to hook with slip knot. Ch 15.

**Base row forward:** Insert hook in second chain from hook. Wrap yarn around the hook and pull the loop through. Repeat with each chain to the end. Do not turn. You should have 15 loops on the hook.

**Base row reverse:** Yo and pull through 1 loop, just like you are making a ch. *Wrap yo and pull through 2 loops. Repeat from * to end; you will have pulled through 2 loops a total of 14 times. 1 loop will remain on hook.

**Tss forward row:** Insert hook from right to left under the second vertical thread below, keeping the hook to the front of the work (not poking through to the back). Yo and pull through, keeping the loop on the hook. *Insert hook under the next vertical thread. Yo and pull through. Repeat from * to end of row. This creates the forward row of Tunisian simple stitch. You should have 15 loops on the hook at the end of each forward row.

**Tss reverse row:** Same as base row reverse.

Continue to work Tss forward and reverse rows until scarf is desired length, approximately 50 inches long. Do not fasten off.

**Tip:** It is essential to keep the same number of stitches on each row. Because the loops stay on the hook like in knitting, it is possible to "drop" a stitch accidentally or to pull the yarn through too few or too many loops on a reverse row. Periodically count the stitches to make sure you are consistent.

**Trim:** Ch 1. Sc in first sp between vertical bars across short end of scarf. 3 sc in corner. (If this makes the corner look too crowded, just work 2 sc in corner.) Sc down long side, 1 stitch at the end of every row. Work 2 or 3 sc in corner as in previous corner. Sc in each st across bottom. Work corner and other long side back to where you started the trim. If you worked 3 sc in other corners, work 2 sc in the corner where you started; if you worked 2 sc in the other corners, just work 1 sc in starting corner. Join with sl st to first ch. Fasten off.

**Finishing:** Steam block by using a steam iron on low. Lay the scarf flat on the ironing board. Hover the iron just above the scarf, being careful not to press down on the stitches. Let the steam penetrate the stitches. Flip the scarf over and steam the other side. Pay particular attention to the ends, steaming them thoroughly.

**Tip:** In Tunisian simple stitch, the ends can tend to curl. Steam blocking minimizes this curl. Roll your scarf in the opposite direction of the curl from both ends, like a scroll, when you store it. This also helps to alleviate the curl.

Each row is worked in 2 passes. The first pass, called "forward," goes from right to left and adds loops onto the hook. The second pass, called "reverse," moves from left to right and removes loops from the hook. (Left-handers will work in the opposite direction.)

The first row is called the base row. It is worked into the foundation chains.

**1.** Attach yarn to hook with a slip knot. Make the specified number of ch stitches.

**2.** Find the second chain from the hook. Do not count the stitch that the hook is in.

**3.** Push the hook through the chain from front to back.

**4.** Wrap yarn over and pull to the front. There will be 2 loops on the hook. This starts the forward pass of the base row.

**5.** Continue across in this fashion, adding a loop to the hook with every stitch. Make sure you do this on the final chain—don't leave it out or you will not have enough stitches.

At the end of the row, count to make sure the number of loops on the hook is the same as the number of chains you made to get started. This completes the forward pass of the base row.

**6.** Do not turn. Now you will start the reverse pass of the base row. Yo and pull through 1 loop, like you are making a chain stitch.

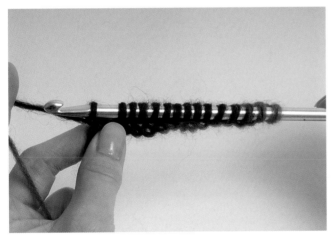

**7.** Yarn over and pull through 2 loops.

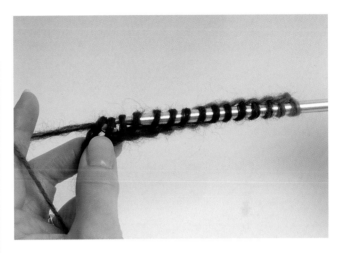

Continue in this fashion (yo and pulling through 2 loops) to the end of the base row. You should end up with just 1 loop on the hook.

Look at the completed row of stitches. You will see a vertical bar for each stitch. These bars are what you will pick up as you work the Tunisian simple stitch forward pass.

**8.** Skip the vertical bar that is on the far right side of the piece, right under the hook. Put the hook through the next vertical bar from right to left. Keep the hook to the front of the work, not poking through to the back.

Wrap the yarn over and pull to the front. There will be 2 loops on the hook, like in the forward pass of the base row.

**9.** Continue across in this fashion, adding a loop to the hook with every stitch.

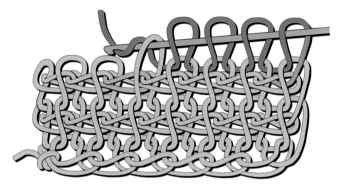

At the end of the row, pick up the vertical bar on the far left. Count to make sure the number of loops on the hook is the same as the number of stitches in the base row and the number of ch you started with. This completes the forward pass of the Tunisian simple stitch.

**10.** Do not turn. Now you will start the reverse pass of the Tunisian simple stitch. Wrap the yarn over the hook and pull through 1 loop, like you are making a chain stitch.

**11.** Wrap the yarn over the hook and pull through 2 loops. Continue in this fashion, yo and pulling through 2 loops, to the end of the row. You should end up with just 1 loop on the hook.

Continue in this fashion, working the forward and reverse rows of Tunisian simple stitch. After a few rows, turn the fabric over to see how different the back looks from the front.

**1.** Complete Tss until your scarf is the desired length. Do not fasten off.

**2.** Ch 1. This counts as 1 sc.

**3.** Work 1 sc in each stitch going across the short end of the scarf.

**4.** In the corner, work 2 or 3 sc, whichever looks neater.

**5.** Work sc down the long side, into the corner, across the bottom, in the third corner, and up the other long side. If you made 2 sc in the corners, work 1 sc in the corner where you started; if you made 3 sc in the corners, work 2 sc in the corner where you started.

**6.** Join to top of first ch with sl st.

**7.** Fasten off.

Tunisian crochet has a hazard well-known to knitters: it is possible to "drop" a stitch either by inadvertently skipping a vertical bar on a forward row or by pulling through the wrong number of loops on the return row. If you count your stitches frequently, you will discover any errors almost immediately and will be able to correct them. Here's how.

**1.** Identify the place where the stitch was missed. Here, the crocheter is on the return row and sees that a vertical bar was missed.

**2.** Remove the hook from the working yarn. Keep the other loops on the hook.

**3.** Gently pull the yarn out from the return row and from the forward row until you get to the bar you missed.

**4.** Pick up the missed bar and continue with the forward row.

Unfortunately there is no good way to work a dropped stitch up through subsequent rows. You will have to rip out stitches until you get back to the error.

**Tunisian Crochet Scarf**

# 3

# Diagonal Pillow

Working on the diagonal eliminates the need for a long foundation chain. The pattern begins with just 6 chains to start a block in one corner. Blocks are added along both sides in a stepwise, triangular pattern until the maximum diagonal is attained and then decreased at the same rate to form a square. Variegated yarn shows off the diagonal technique to great advantage.

Tassels in each corner dress up this classy, cozy pillow. Make a few pillows in different color schemes and switch them when the seasons change for an instant decorating lift.

**Finished size:** 16 inches square, plus 2-inch-long tassel in each corner

## Materials:

James C. Brett Marble yarn (100 percent acrylic, 100 grams/3.5 ounces, 240 yards/220 meters)

2 skeins color MT8

Hook: G or size necessary to obtain gauge

16-inch square machine washable pillow form

## Stitches and abbreviations:

Chain stitch (ch)

Double crochet (dc)

Reverse single crochet (rsc)

Slip stitch (sl st)

## Gauge:

6 diagonal blocks in a line (3 run horizontally, 3 are oriented vertically)/4 inches. Gauge is important so the pillow top and bottom fit over the form properly.

**Tip:** Pillow forms come in different colors. Choose one that is closest to the color scheme for your pillow so it will not show through.

## Pillow Top (make 2)

Attach yarn to hook with slip knot. Ch 6.

**First block:** Skip first 3 ch. Work 1 dc in fourth ch from hook and in each of next 2 ch. Total 4 dc (including turning ch).

**Second row of blocks:** Ch 6. Work 1 dc in fourth, fifth, and sixth ch from hook. Flip up the first block so the dc stitches are perpendicular to the ones you just made. The ch may look twisted—this is okay. Sl st into the space below the top dc. Ch 3 (this counts as a dc). 3 dc into space below the top dc where you made the sl st. 2 blocks made on this row for a total of 3 blocks.

**Tip:** The dc stitches in each block should run perpendicular to the stitches in the adjoining blocks.

**Third row of blocks:** Ch 6. Work 1 dc in fourth, fifth, and sixth ch from hook. Flip up the completed 3 blocks so the dc stitches are perpendicular to the ones you just made. The ch may look twisted—this is okay. *Sl st into the space below the top dc in the adjoining block. Ch 3 (this counts as a dc). 3 dc into space below the top dc where you made the sl st. Repeat from * 2 more times. 3 blocks made for a total of 6 blocks.

**Rows 4–25:** Continue increasing in this manner. Row 25 should be the longest row you need for the pillow, extending 16 inches across and 16 inches up. Test your pillow top against the pillow form to make sure it is the right size. If necessary, continue increasing until the pillow top is the right size. Now you will begin to decrease the number of blocks per row.

**Row 26:** Ch 3. Turn. Line the chains up along the dc from the previous block. *Sl st into the space below the top dc from the previous block. Ch 3 (this counts as a dc). 3 dc into the space below the top dc. Repeat from * up the "steps" of the blocks until 1 block remains. Sl st into the space at the upper right corner of the block to complete the row.

**Rows 27–48:** Repeat row 26.

**Tip:** Periodically lay the pillow top on top of the form to check the size.

**Row 49:** Ch 3. Line up the chains along the dc from the previous block. Sl st into the space below the top dc. Ch 3 (this counts as a dc). 3 dc into the space below the top dc. Sl st into the space below the top dc of the next block. Fasten off.

Make 4 tassels. (See Skill Workshop.)

**Finishing and assembly:** Weave in ends. Steam block both pieces to get the corners sharp and the edges straight.

**1.** Lay one of the squares right side down and the other square right side up on top of it. Orient the squares so the diagonals go the same direction. You may leave the sides loose, gathering them together as you go along, or pin in place.

Diagonal Pillow

**2.** Using long yarn from top of 1 tassel, attach tassel by pulling the ends through adjacent stitches in the corner of the bottom pillow square. Tie securely and weave ends in.

**3.** To begin closing the pillow top and bottom, join yarn by working 1 sc through both thicknesses of a corner. Work reverse single crochet (moving to the right) around the perimeter of the pillow.

**4.** As you get to each corner, attach the tassel before closing that corner. Work 2 or 3 rsc (see Skill Workshop) in each corner to make the corner square.

**5.** After you close 3 sides of the pillow, slide the pillow form in.

Continue working in rsc to close the remaining side.

**6.** When you get back to the beginning, work 1 or 2 more rsc to make that corner square. Join to top of first sc with a sl st. Fasten off. Pull end through to inside of pillow.

The diagonal arrangement of stitches works well for any square or other rectangle. It eliminates the need to make a long foundation chain. The way blocks are added and decreased determines the size and shape of the fabric. The pillow is made of 2 squares worked in double crochet on the diagonal.

**Row 1 (block 1):** Attach yarn to hook with a slip knot. Ch 6.

Count back to find the fourth ch from the hook. Work 1 dc in that ch and in the next 2 ch. This makes a square of 4 dc. (The 3 unworked ch count as the fourth one here and throughout the pattern.)

**Row 2 (blocks 2 and 3):** Ch 6. Again, count back to find the fourth ch from the hook. Work 1 dc in that ch and in the next 2 ch. This makes another square of 4 dc.

Now flip up block 1 so the stitches from that block run perpendicular to the stitches you just made. Nestle it right next to the new block.

Join the blocks by working a sl st in the space below the 3 ch in block 1.

Ch 3, which counts as a dc. Work 3 more dc into the same space. Now you have 3 squares.

**Row 3 (blocks 4, 5, and 6):** Ch 6. Work 1 ch in the fourth ch from the hook and in the next 2 ch.

This makes block 4.

Flip up the previously completed blocks so the stitches from block 3 run perpendicular to the ones you just made for block 4. Nestle the blocks right next to each other. Join the blocks by working a sl st in the space below the 3 ch in block 3.

*Ch 3, which counts as a dc. Work 3 more dc into the same space. This completes block 5. Join with a sl st to block 2.

Repeat from *. This completes block 6.

Continue in this fashion until the side and bottom of the pillow top measure 16 inches each. You will see the pillow top grow in a stepwise fashion.

To decrease after pillow has reached its maximum diagonal and you want to start getting smaller, ch 3 (not 6). Turn.

Lay the 3 ch along the top of the just-completed block. Sl st in the space under the top stitch in that block. *Ch 3, which counts as a dc.

Work 3 dc into the same space where you did the sl st. Sl st to join to top of next block.

Repeat from * until you get to the last block. Join with a sl st. Ch 3, but do not work any dc in that final block. Turn the work, lay the 3 ch along the top of the just-completed block, and continue in the decrease pattern.

This decreases each row at each end, creating a square.

Reverse single crochet is worked like a standard single crochet, except the stitches go from left to right (for left-handers, reverse sc goes from right to left). Also known as corded single crochet or crab stitch, it gives a twist to each stitch, creating an attractive corded edge.

**1.** After attaching the yarn to the pillow corner with a regular single crochet, insert the hook in the next stitch to the right. Point the hook downward to get it through the stitch more easily.

Remember to go through both thicknesses, the top and the bottom of the pillow. Wrap yarn over and pull to the front.

Yo and pull through both loops to complete the stitch.

**2.** Continuing to the right, work 1 rsc into each st from previous row.

Diagonal Pillow

**1.** Cut a piece of cardboard 6 inches long. Lay a 12-inch piece of yarn across the top.

**2.** Starting at the bottom of the cardboard, wrap the yarn around the cardboard and over the long piece of yarn 20 times.

Cut the yarn so the end is flush with the bottom of the cardboard.

**Tip:** Do not cut all the loops yet, just the end of the yarn you finished wrapping.

**3.** Using the long piece of yarn you initially laid at the top of the cardboard, tie a knot to hold the yarn in a bundle. Do not trim the yarn—you will use this to attach the tassel to the corner of the pillow.

**4.** Cut the yarn across the bottom of the cardboard.

**5.** Using another 12-inch piece of yarn, tie the bundle about 1 inch below the top. Make a nice firm knot.

**6.** Trim all ends of tassel, including the pieces you just used to make the knot 1 inch below the top, to the same length.

# 4

# Lacy Wire Necklace

Crocheted wire makes gorgeous jewelry. Wire comes in a rainbow of colors and is easy to work with after just a little practice. Once you are comfortable with the feel, you will be able to make fashionable accessories for yourself and to give as gifts.

**Finished size:** 18 inches long, plus ½ inch for closure. You can adjust the size by making the first row longer or shorter.

**Materials:**

Artistic wire, colored copper wire, 30 gauge (30 yards/27 meters on a spool):

Color A: dark blue, #03b, 1 spool

Artistic wire, silver-plated colored copper wire, 30 gauge (30 yards/27 meters on a spool):

Color B: rose, #02, 1 spool

Color C: seafoam green, #09, 1 spool

or

Artistic wire, silver-plated colored copper wire, 30 gauge (30 yards/27 meters on a spool):

Color A: fuschia, #15, 1 spool

Color B: tangerine, #11, 1 spool

Color C: lemon, #12, 1 spool

**Note:** The first color series represents the necklace being made in the skill workshop. The second color series identifies completed wire necklace on the model.

**Tip:** Wire gauge refers to its thickness. The lower the number, the thicker it is. Very thick wire is hard to work with; very thin wire breaks easily. The ideal gauge for wire to crochet is from 28 to 32.

Hooks: Size F (3.75 mm) and Size E (3.50 mm)

Jump rings, 1 set (available at craft stores)

Jewelry clasp, 1 set (available at craft stores)

Stitch marker

Wire cutter or scissors

Pliers, needle-nose or chain-nose style for attaching closures

Clear nail polish

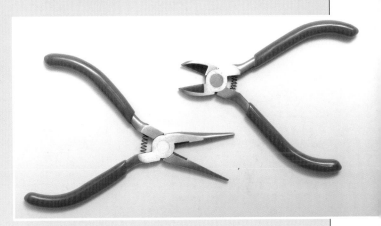

**Tip:** Wire ends are sharp. When you cut wire, wear eye protection or shield the area being cut so there is no danger of a shard hitting your eyes or the eyes of anyone around you. Dispose of all cuttings promptly.

Put a dab of clear nail polish on all wire ends when your project is finished. This helps prevent the wire from poking the wearer.

**Stitches and abbreviations:**

Chain stitch (ch)

Double crochet (dc)

Half double crochet (hdc)

Slip stitch (sl st)

Skip (sk)

Stitch or stitches (st or sts)

**Gauge** (crocheted gauge, not wire gauge):

Does not matter for this project.

# Wire Necklace

Measure around the neck to determine the length of the finished necklace. Subtract ¹/₂ inch from this measurement to account for the size of the closure. This leaves the finished measurement for your crocheted piece.

**Tip:** Because wire gets bent and has sharp ends, crocheted wire projects in progress are not the best choice to take on the road. Stuffing these fragile creations into a bag can damage them. Fortunately, jewelry items are small and can be completed quickly, so there is not much need to tote them around.

With colors A and B together and the larger hook, ch a multiple of 6 sts plus 1 to get to your desired length.

**Row 1:** With smaller hook and color A only, work 1 ch into second ch from hook, work 5 hdc into next ch, *sk 1, 1 sl st into each of the next 3 ch, sk 1, 5 hdc into next ch, repeat from * to end of foundation ch, ending with 5 hdc in last ch. Do not turn.

**Row 2:** Starting where you started row 1, but this time using color B only, [1 sl st in center of 5 hdc, sl st in next (previously skipped) st, ch 3, sk 3, 1 sl st in next (previously skipped) st], repeat instructions in [ ] to end of row, ending with 1 sl st in center of final 5 hdc. Do not turn.

**Row 3:** Again returning to where you started, join C in center st of first 5 hdc, *7 dc in 3-ch loop, sl st in center st of next 5 hdc, rep from * to end of row, ending with sl st in center of last 5 hdc.

**Finishing:** Cut wire about 6 inches from end. Pull loose ends through the loop. Twist the ends. Cut this spiral to about a ¹/₂ inch. Coil this twisted strand into a flat disk and press it tightly against the underside of the piece. Dab on some clear nail polish to prevent a wire from scratching the wearer. Do the same thing at the other end of the necklace.

Attach a jump ring to each end of necklace. Attach one end of the clasp to each jump ring. Gently shape and pinch the piece with your hands to smooth the shells and have the necklace lie properly. Shorten any remaining ends. Press them flat against the necklace.

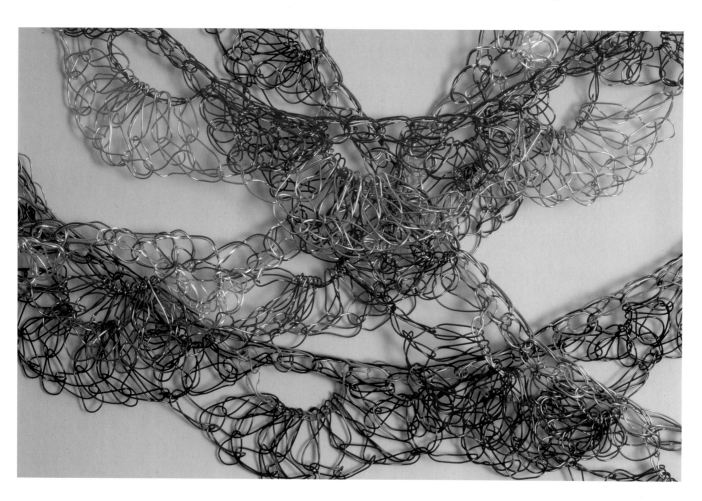

# SKILL WORKSHOP: CROCHETING WITH WIRE

**1.** Use 2 strands of wire (A and B) together and the larger hook. Attach wire to hook with sl st.

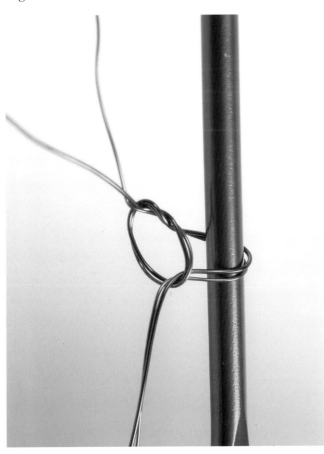

**2.** Foundation row: Ch a multiple of 6 stitches plus 1 extra—for example, (6 x 13) + 1 = 79 stitches—until you get to the desired length for your necklace.

**3.** Row 1: Turn. Switch to smaller hook. You will be working with just color A on this row. Let color B hang; it will not pull out or be in your way. Ch 1.

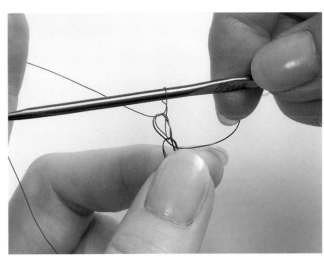

**Tip:** Before you make the necklace, practice crocheting with wire to get used to the way it feels. Use a few different hook sizes, anything from C (2.75 mm) through G (4.25 mm), and several different wire gauges if possible to try out basic stitches like chain, single, half double, double, and slip stitch. The goal is to keep your stitches consistent in size and relatively loose. Bend the finished stitches gently to keep them aligned properly with no twisting.

Wire stitches are harder to take out than those made with yarn. If you need to undo a stitch, gently ease it back through the hole. Do not pull it hard from the other side. Try not to undo stitches or crimp them because this can weaken the wire.

To help the wire flow smoothly off the spool, slip a bead over the end of the wire before you start working.

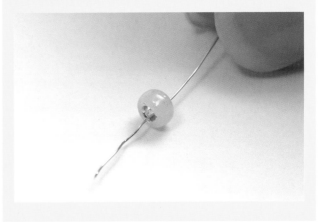

**4.** Work 5 hdc into second ch from hook (the first 2-strand ch).

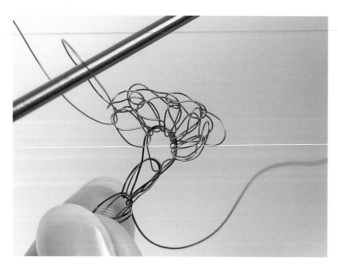

**5.** *Sk 1 ch. Work 1 sl st into each of the next 3 ch. Sk 1 ch. Work 5 hdc into the next ch.

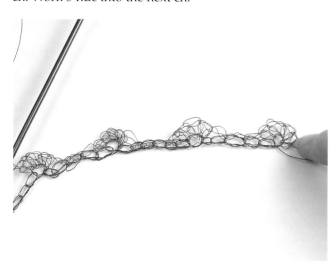

**6.** Repeat from * to end of foundation ch, ending with 5 hdc in the last ch.

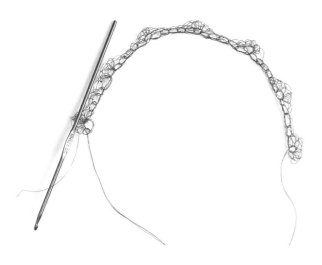

**7.** Remove hook from color A. Insert a stitch marker or bobby pin to keep that loop from undoing.

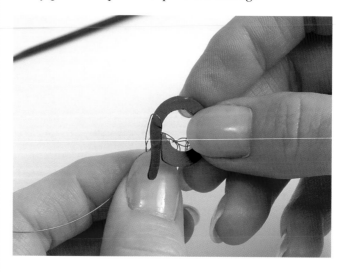

**8.** Row 2: Do not turn. You will work the same direction as row 1. Using the same (smaller) hook, insert hook in color B where you left off at end of foundation row.

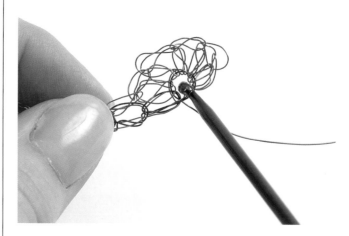

**9.** Work 1 sl st in the arch under the 5 hdc.

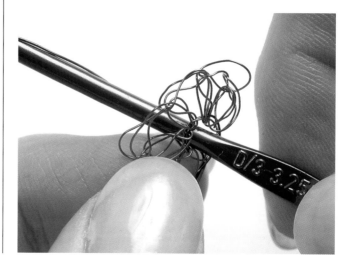

**10.** Sl st in next (previously skipped) st.

**11.** Ch 3 . . .

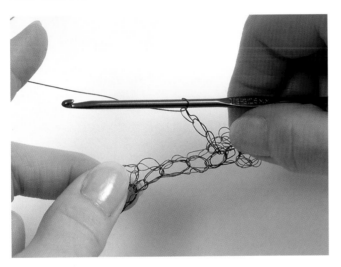

. . . sk 3, 1 sl st in next (previously skipped) st . . .

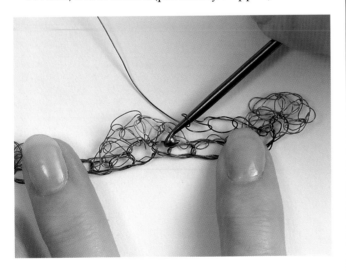

. . . sl st in the arch under the next group of 5 hdc. Continue in this fashion to the end of the row, ending with 1 sl st in the arch under the final 5 hdc.

**12.** Remove hook. Add this loop to the stitch marker to hold both loops in place.

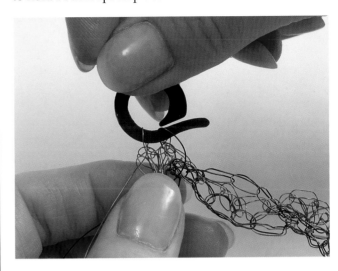

**13.** Row 3: Do not turn. You will work the same direction as rows 1 and 2. Return to beginning of row. Join color C in the third hdc.

**14.** Work 7 dc in the 3-ch loop.

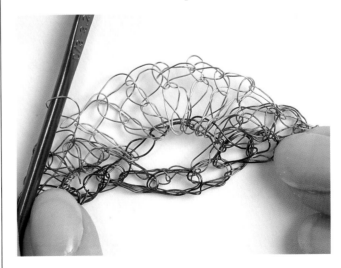

**15.** Sl st in the third hdc of the next group of 5 hdc . . .

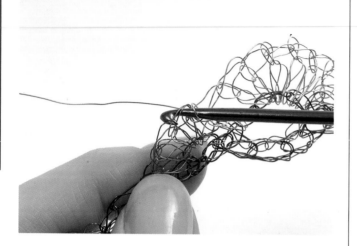

. . . 7 dc in next 3-ch loop. Continue in this pattern to the end of the row, ending with a sl st in the center of the last 5 hdc.

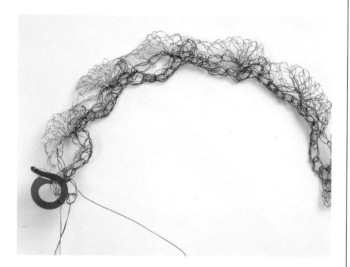

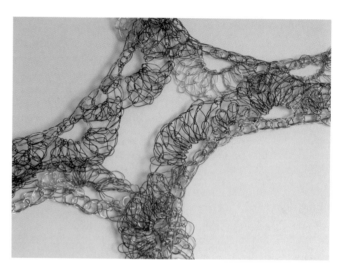

## SKILL WORKSHOP: FINISHING A NECKLACE

Now the crocheting is done, and all that remains is to attach the clasp and work in the ends.

**1.** Cut the wire about 6 inches from the end.

**2.** Pull the ends through the loop of all 3 colors.

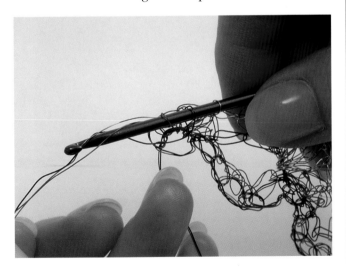

**3.** Twist the ends into a tight spiral. Cut to about a $1/2$-inch.

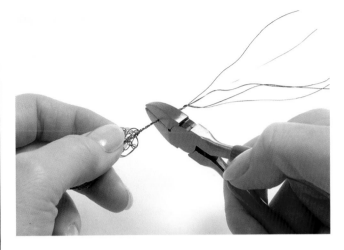

**4.** Coil this twisted strand into a flat disk.

**5.** Press it very tightly against the underside of the necklace.

**6.** Work the wire at the other end through an adjacent stitch a few times to secure it.

**7.** Dab on a little clear nail polish to prevent a loose wire from scratching the wearer.

**8.** Select a jump ring. If it is this kind, open it gently. You will place one of these at each end of the necklace to connect the wire to the clasp.

**9.** Hook the jump ring through several loops of wire.

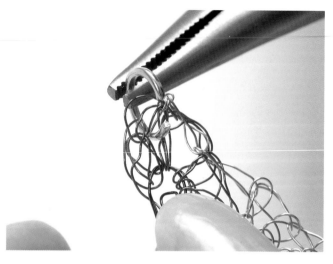

**Tip:** Jump rings come in different styles. This one is a coil. Attach it by sliding one end over several loops of wire, then working it around until the entire coil is attached to the wire.

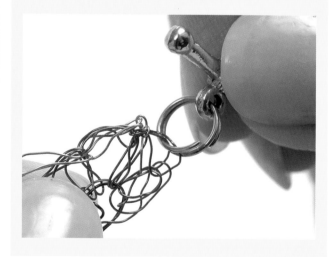

**10.** Attach the clasp to the jump ring. If you are using a lobster clasp, you may not need to do anything on the other end, as long as the clasp can hook onto the jump ring. If the ring at the other end is too small, attach a larger ring for the clasp to attach to.

**11.** Close the jump ring with the pliers if necessary (if it is not the coil type). Make sure the ends line up.

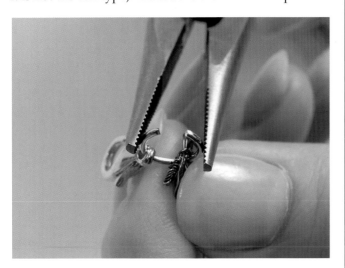

If you are using a toggle clasp, attach one end to each jump ring.

**12.** Gently shape and pinch the piece with your hands to smooth the stitches and have the necklace lie properly.

# 5

# Bunny Rabbit

This cute and cuddly rabbit makes friends wherever he hops. The head and body are worked in 1 piece for ease and stability. Facial features are embroidered so there are no small plastic pieces like eyes or whiskers that could break off and present a choking hazard. Pair the bunny with the basket from *Basic Crocheting* for a delightful Easter duo.

**Finished size:** Approximately 16 inches tall to top of ear

## Materials:

Yarn:

Lion Brand Baby Soft sport weight yarn (459 yards/420 meters):

1 skein pastel yellow (157)

1 skein lavender (143)

Lion Brand Baby Soft sport weight pompadour yarn (367 yards/335 meters):

1 skein baby pink (201)

Hooks:

Size H (5.00 mm) or size needed for gauge

Size E (3.50 mm) or whatever size is 1.5 mm smaller than other hook

Polyester fiberfill, 10 ounces

Stitch markers (2)

Tapestry needle

Straight pins to hold pieces in place

2 cardboard circles, approximately 3³/₄ inches in diameter, for pompon making

Decorative ribbon, 1 inch wide by 40 inches long

## Gauge:

Work the pattern through round 3. Swatch should be 2 inches in diameter.

## Stitches and abbreviations:

Back loop only (blo)

Chain stitch (ch)

Decrease (dec)

Single crochet (sc)

Slip stitch (sl st)

2 single crochet together (2 sc tog)

Yarn over (yo)

To work a decreasing sc, also known as working 2 sc tog, pull up 1 loop in the next stitch but do not complete the stitch. Instead, insert the hook in the next stitch and pull up a loop. Yo and draw through all 3 loops on the hook. This counts as 1 sc.

**Tip:** Stitch markers are used to identify the beginning or end of each round and to identify the ends of ovals on the feet. Place marker in the top of a completed stitch as instructed in the pattern. When you complete the next round, move the marker.

**Tip:** Keep a pencil handy so you can mark down the row you stopped on if you take a break.

## Bunny Rabbit Head and Body

**Round 1 (starts head):** With yellow, using larger hook, ch 2. In second ch from hook, work 8 sc. This forms a circle. Do not join. Place marker in last st made.

**Round 2:** 2 sc in each sc around: 16 sc. Move marker to end of round just completed, now and throughout.

**Round 3:** (Sc in next sc, 2 sc in next sc) around: 24 sc.

**Round 4:** (Sc in next 2 sc, 2 sc in next sc) around: 32 sc.

**Round 5:** (Sc in next 7 sc, 2 sc in next sc) around: 36 sc.

**Round 6:** Sc in each sc around: 36 sc.

**Round 7:** (Sc in next 5 sc, 2 sc in next sc) around: 42 sc.

**Rounds 8–9:** Sc in each sc around: 42 sc.

**Round 10:** (Sc in next 6 sc, 2 sc in next sc) around: 48 sc.

**Rounds 11–17:** Sc in each sc around: 48 sc.

**Tip:** Make sure you work all of the rounds. Do not accidentally skip from round 11 to round 18.

**Round 18:** (Sc in next 6 sc, dec by working 2 sc tog) around: 42 sc.

**Rounds 19–20:** Sc in each sc around: 42 sc.

**Round 21:** (Sc in next 5 sc, dec) around: 36 sc.

**Round 22:** Sc in each sc around: 36 sc.

**Round 23:** (Sc in next 7 sc, dec) around: 32 sc.

**Round 24:** Sc in each sc around: 32 sc.

**Round 25:** (Sc in next 2 sc, dec) around: 24 sc.

**Round 26:** Sc in each sc around: 24 sc. Do not fasten off.

**Tip:** Take your hook out and put a stitch marker into the loop to keep stitches from pulling out as you stuff the bunny's head.

Stuff the head with polyester fiberfill until the head is quite firm, but the stitches are not stretched too much.

**Round 27:** Dec all around: 12 sc.

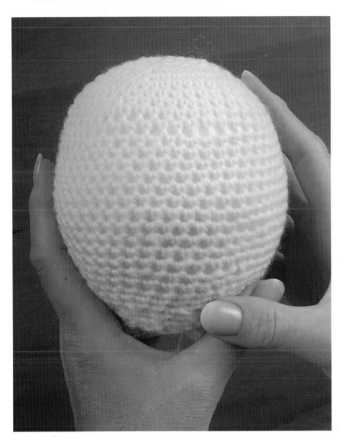

**Round 28 (starts body):** 2 sc in each sc around: 24 sc.

**Round 29:** (Sc in next 2 sc, 2 sc in next sc) around: 32 sc.

**Round 30:** (Sc in next 7 sc, 2 sc in next sc) around: 36 sc.

**Round 31:** Sc in each sc around: 36 sc.

**Round 32:** (Sc in next 5 sc, 2 sc in next sc) around: 42 sc.

**Round 33:** Sc in each sc around: 42 sc.

**Round 34:** (Sc in next 6 sc, 2 sc in next sc) around: 48 sc.

**Round 35:** Sc in each sc around: 48 sc.

**Round 36:** (Sc in next 7 sc, 2 sc in next sc) around: 54 sc.

**Round 37:** Sc in each sc around: 54 sc.

**Round 38:** (Sc in next 8 sc, 2 sc in next sc) around: 60 sc.

**Rounds 39–40:** Sc in each sc around: 60 sc.

**Round 41:** (Sc in next 11 sc, 2 sc in next sc) around: 65 sc.

**Rounds 42–44:** Sc in each sc around: 65 sc.

**Round 45:** (Sc in next 12 sc, 2 sc in next sc) around: 70 sc.

**Rounds 46–47:** Sc in each sc around: 70 sc.

**Round 48:** (Sc in next 9 sc, 2 sc in next sc) around: 77 sc.

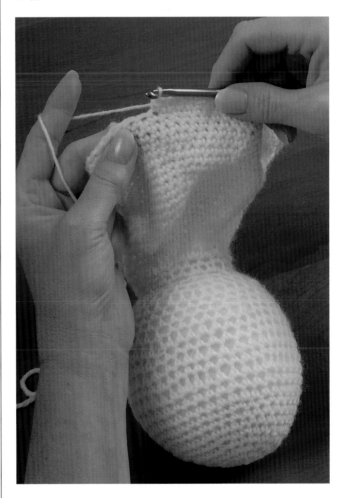

**Rounds 49–51:** Sc in each sc around: 77 sc.

**Round 52:** (Sc in next 10 sc, 2 sc in next sc) around: 84 sc.

**Rounds 53–55:** Sc in each sc around: 84 sc.

**Round 56:** (Sc in next 11 sc, 2 sc in next sc) around: 91 sc.

**Rounds 57–59:** Sc in each sc around: 91 sc.

**Round 60:** (Sc in next 12 sc, 2 sc in next sc) around: 98 sc.

**Rounds 61–63:** Sc in each sc around: 98 sc.

**Round 64:** (Sc in next 13 sc, 2 sc in next sc) around: 105 sc.

**Rounds 65–68:** Sc in each sc around: 105 sc.

**Round 69:** (Sc in next 13 sc, dec) around: 98 sc.

**Round 70:** Sc in each sc around: 98 sc.

**Round 71:** (Sc in next 5 sc, dec) around: 84 sc.

**Round 72:** Sc in each sc around: 84 sc.

**Round 73:** (Sc in next 5 sc, dec) around: 72 sc.

**Round 74:** Sc in each sc around: 72 sc.

**Round 75:** (Sc in next 4 sc, dec) around: 60 sc.

**Round 76:** Sc in each sc around: 60 sc.

**Round 77:** (Sc in next 3 sc, dec) around: 48 sc.

**Round 78:** Sc in each sc around: 48 sc.

**Round 79:** (Sc in next 2 sc, dec) around: 36 sc.

**Round 80:** Sc in each sc around: 36 sc.

**Round 81:** (Sc in next sc, dec) around: 24 sc.

**Round 82:** Sc in each sc around: 24 sc.

Stuff body with fiberfill until firm. As you work the rest of the body to completion, add stuffing as needed. Look at the head and body from above to make sure they are nice and round, and the head is not floppy.

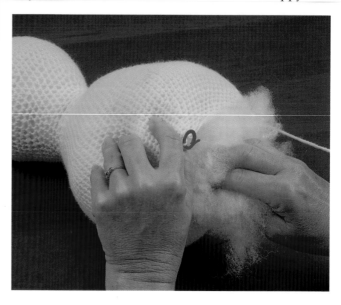

**Round 83:** Dec around: 12 sc.

**Round 84:** Sc in each sc around: 12 sc.

**Round 85:** Dec around: 6 sc.

Fasten off, leaving a long tail. Thread the tail onto a tapestry needle. Pick up each stitch around the bottom of the body. Sew closed.

Your bunny will look a lot like a bowling pin.

## Back Foot (make 2)

With yellow and larger hook, ch 6.

**Round 1:** Starting with second ch from hook, work 1 sc in top loop only in that st and in the next 3 ch. Work 3 sc into next ch, placing a stitch marker in the second of those 3 sc. Now you will come back around the other side of the original chs. Work 1 sc in each free loop of the next 3 ch and then work 2 sc into the last ch. This makes a small oval. Total 12 sc. Do not join. Place second marker so it is exactly opposite the first marker. The markers indicate the ends of the ovals, where you will work the increases.

**Round 2:** Continuing in spiral fashion, work 1 sc into each st (both loops) until you reach the marker at the other end. Work 3 sc into the stitch that holds the marker. Move marker to the second of the 3 sc you just made. Continuing down the other side, work 1 sc in each sc and then 2 sc into last sc. Total 16 sc.

**Note:** The markers should now be at the far ends of the oval you just made. Each one should be in the middle of the 3 sc that are worked into 1 st from the previous round. Rounds are increased by 4 stitches each round, 2 at each end (1 on either side of marked stitch).

**Round 3:** Repeat round 2, increasing oval at each end. Total 20 sc.

**Round 4:** Repeat round 2, increasing oval at each end. Total 24 sc.

**Round 5:** Repeat round 2, increasing oval at each end. Total 28 sc.

**Round 6:** Now the increases are finished. Work 1 sc in each sc around. Total 28 sc. Continue to place marker at the end of every round.

**Rounds 7–24:** Repeat round 6. Do not fasten off.

Stuff foot firmly, but make sure the final 4 rounds are not too full. This part of the foot will need to be flattened and sewn to the body.

## Front Foot (make 2)

Work the same as for back foot, but stop at the end of round 20.

## Ear (make 2)

See Skill Workshop.

## Tail

**1.** Cut 2 circles of cardboard approximately $3^3/4$ inches in diameter. Find the center of each circle. Cut a smaller hole, approximately $1^1/2$ inches in diameter, in the center of each cardboard.

**2.** Cut equal lengths of lavender, yellow, and pink yarn, approximately a yard long. Hold the 2 cardboard circles together and wind yarn around the ring. Continue with additional strands of yarn until the circles are completely covered. Make it nice and thick.

**3.** Holding firmly, cut around the outside edge between the 2 circles. Make sure all of the yarn is cut.

**4.** Cut a length of yellow yarn approximately 20 inches long. Separate the 2 cardboard circles slightly. Slip the length of yarn between the circles. Tie into a tight knot. Pull the cardboard gently away. Fluff into a round pompon. Trim as desired, but leave long tails of the tie-yarn for attaching the tail to the body.

## Face

With lavender, use a tapestry needle to embroider the rabbit's nose, mouth, teeth, and whiskers.

**Tip:** To secure the thread, knot the yarn and push the needle from the side of the head to the front where you will sew the face. After the face is completed, cut the knot off and let the end disappear inside the head.

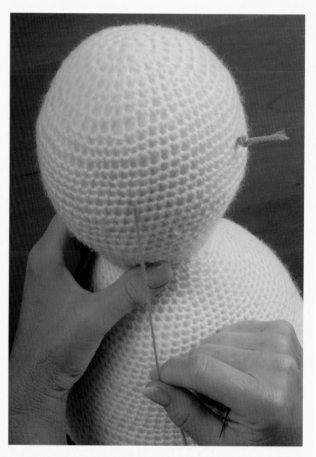

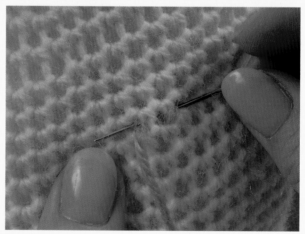

## Eye (make 2)

With lavender and larger hook, ch 2. Work 8 sc into the first sc made. Join ring with sl st. Fasten off.

(If you want a larger eye, work 2 sc into each sc from the first round.) Pin eyes in place. Sew on with lavender, using a tapestry needle. Pull ends through to inside of head.

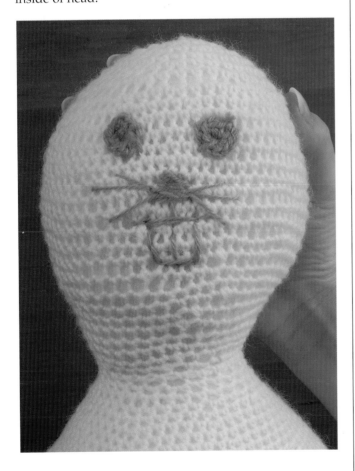

## Assembly

**1.** Pin feet in place. Sew on with a tapestry needle and yellow yarn. Sew 2 rows of stitches (parallel to each other) on each foot, one at the end of the foot and another a $1/2$ inch closer to the toes. This keeps the foot from flopping around.

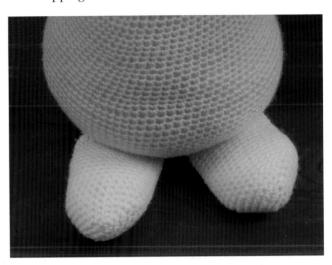

**2.** Pin ears in place, pinching the bottom a little to give them the right shape. Ears are not stuffed. Sew on with a tapestry needle and a length of yellow yarn.

**3.** Position tail. Use crochet hook to pull ends of tie into the body, then out again where tail will hide them. Tie the ends together tightly. Trim so they are the same length as the pompon yarn.

**4.** Tie ribbon in a bow around rabbit's neck.

**5.** Pull any remaining loose yarn ends into the rabbit, making sure they are not visible.

**Bunny Rabbit**

## Ear (make 2)

Switch to smaller hook. Tight stitches give the ear stability so it does not need to be stuffed. Pink part of ear is worked from bottom to top, then the yellow is worked around the edges and the back.

With pink, ch 9.

**Row 1:** Sc in third ch from hook and in each ch across. Total 8 sc including turning ch.

**Row 2:** Ch 2. Turn. Do not work into base of turning ch (the 2 ch you made count as the first sc). Work 1 sc in each sc across, including in top of turning ch from previous row. Total 8 sc.

**Rows 3–6:** Repeat row 2.

**Row 7:** Ch 2. Turn. Work 1 sc into base of turning ch to increase, 1 sc in each sc across, then 2 sc in top of turning ch at other end for another increase. Total 10 sc.

**Rows 8–16:** Repeat row 2. Total 10 sc.

**Row 17:** Ch 2. Turn. Do not work into base of turning ch. Work 1 sc across until 2 st remain. Work those 2 sc tog into 1 sc. Total 9 sc.

**Row 18:** Repeat row 11. Total 8 sc.

**Row 19:** Repeat row 11. Total 7 sc.

**Row 20:** Repeat row 11. Total 6 sc.

**Row 21:** Repeat row 11. Total 5 sc.

**Row 22:** Repeat row 11. Total 4 sc.

Fasten off.

## Outer Ear

**Round 1:** With right side of inner ear facing you, use smaller hook to join yellow to bottom corner where you started the ear. Work sc evenly up one side of ear, around the top, and down the other side. Do not work sc across the bottom. Total 44 sc.

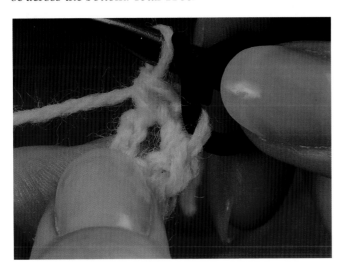

**Round 2:** Ch 2. Turn. Work 1 sc in each sc around. Total 44 sc.

**Round 3:** Ch 2. Turn. Work 1 sc in blo of each sc around. Total 44 sc.

**Tip:** Working in the blo (back loop only) on this round starts the back part of the ear. As you continue, the edges of the ear will get closer together until eventually you will join them to complete the back of the ear.

**Round 4:** Ch 2. Turn. Work 1 sc in both loops of each sc around. Total 44 sc.

**Round 5:** Ch 2. Turn. Work 1 sc in each sc until you reach the crest of the ear. Work 2 sc tog into 1. Work 11 sc in each sc down the other side of ear. Total 43 dc.

**Round 6:** Repeat round 5. Total 42 dc.

**Round 7:** Repeat round 5. Total 41 sc. Do not fasten off.

Turn so ear is inside out, with right sides on the inside. Line up sides of ear and work a row of sc to join the sides together.

Fasten off. Weave in ends. Turn ear right side out.

76

# 6

# Sassy Socks

Treat your tootsies to a pair of these adorable socks! Ankle shaping and yarn with a bit of stretch make for a great fit. The "afterthought" heel is worked last. The heel and the cuff trim are worked in a contrasting color just for fun.

**Finished shoe size:** XS, S, M, L, XL
(see chart below)

**Materials:**

Cascade Fixation (98.3 percent cotton, 1.7 percent elastic, $1^3/_4$ ounces/50 grams, 100 yards/91 meters)

Yarn A: 2 balls color 9385 key lime

Yarn B: 1 ball color 2550 lapis

Hooks: E/3.50 mm or size necessary to obtain gauge; also D/3.25 mm (or one size smaller than the hook that meets the gauge requirements)

Stitch marker

Tapestry needle

**Gauge:**

Using larger hook, 5 sc/1 inch; 6 sc rows/ 1 inch

**Stitches and abbreviations:**

Back loop only (blo)

Chain stitch (ch)

Repeat (rep)

Single crochet (sc)

Single crochet 3 together (sc 3 tog)

Single crochet 2 together (sc 2 tog)

Slip stitch (sl st)

Stitch (st)

Yarn over (yo)

**Tip:** In the instructions, the first number of stitches is for size XS. The numbers for larger sizes are given in parentheses. For example:

Ch 12 (16, 20, 20, 25)

means to make 12 ch for size XS, 16 for size S, 20 for size M, 20 for size L, and 25 for size XL. In this pattern, sometimes 2 sizes have the same number of stitches, such as M and L in the example, because the size of that part of the sock is the same for both. Before you start making the socks, go through the pattern and circle in pencil the numbers for your desired size. This will help you avoid mixing sizes accidentally by reading the wrong number.

To single crochet 2 together (sc 2 tog), insert hook in next st. Yo and pull up the loop but do not complete the stitch. Insert hook into next st. Yo and pull up the loop. Yo and pull through all 3 loops on hook. This completes the sc 2 tog. It is the same as a single crochet decrease.

To single crochet 3 together (sc 3 tog), insert hook in next st. Yo and pull up the loop but do not complete the stitch. Insert hook into next st. Yo and pull up the loop but do not complete this stitch either. Insert hook into next st. Yo and pull up the loop. Yo and pull through all 4 loops on hook. This completes the sc 3 tog.

| Finished Shoe Size | | | | | |
|---|---|---|---|---|---|
| | | Foot Length | Cuff Length | Foot Circum. | Heel Height |
| XS | Child size 2 | $7^1/_2$ | 7 | 7 | $2^1/_4$ |
| S | Child $4^1/_2$ / Women's 6 | $8^1/_2$ | $7^3/_4$ | $7^3/_4$ | $2^1/_4$ |
| M | Men's 7 / Women's $8^1/_2$ | $9^1/_2$ | $8^1/_4$ | $8^1/_2$ | $2^3/_4$ |
| L | Men's $9^1/_2$ / Women's 11 | $10^1/_2$ | 9 | $9^1/_4$ | $3^1/_4$ |
| XL | Men's 14 | $11^1/_2$ | $9^1/_2$ | 10 | $3^1/_2$ |
| If you are between sizes, make the next larger size. | | | | | |

## Sock (make 2)

The sock starts at the toe with a sl st loop to create a ring with a closed center.

Use larger hook and color A. Create a sl st loop. Work 6 sc into the loop. Join to first sc with sl st. Pull ring tight to close hole.

**Round 1:** Working in the back loop only (blo) of each st, work 2 sc into each st. Total 12 sc. Do not join. From this point you will work in a spiral with no join at the end of each round. Use a stitch marker in the final stitch of a round to mark the end of that round. Move the marker into its new position after completing each round.

**Round 2:** Repeat round 1. Total 24 sc. Size XS, skip to round 6.

**Round 3:** Continuing to work in blo, *sc 2, work 2 sc into next st, repeat from * to end of round. Total 24 (32, 32, 32, 32) sc. Size S, skip to round 6.

**Round 4 (sizes M, L, and XL only):** Continuing to work in blo, * sc 3, work 2 sc into next st, repeat from * to end of round. Total 24 (32, 40, 40, 40) sc. Sizes M and L, skip to round 6.

**Round 5 (size XL only):** Continuing to work in blo, * sc 3, work 2 sc into next st, repeat from * to end of round. Total 24 (32, 40, 40, 50) sc.

**Round 6 (all sizes):** Continuing to work in blo, 1 sc in each st. Total 24 (32, 40, 40, 50) sc.

Repeat round 6 with no increases until the sock is long enough to reach the ankle bone, approximately $5^1/_4$, 6, $6^3/_4$, $7^1/_4$, 8 inches, or desired length to heel.

## Afterthought Heel Placement

Ch 12 (16, 20, 20, 25) st. Sk the same number of stitches as the number of ch. Working in blo, sc into next 12 (16, 20, 20, 25) st. Place marker at center of chains to mark the center back of sock.

> **Tip:** Using a smaller hook and working decrease sc (2 sc tog) where indicated will indent the ankle and give it a nice fitted shape.

## Ankle Shaping and Leg

**Round 1:** Work 1 sc into each ch from previous round. Sc into blo of next 12 (16, 20, 20, 25) sts. Total 24 (32, 40, 40, 50) sc. Move marker up to mark center back of sock.

**Round 2:** With smaller hook, work 1 sc in blo. At marker, sc 2 tog. Continue around working 1 sc in blo.

Repeat previous round 2 (3, 4, 4, 5) times. Total 21 (28, 35, 35, 44) sc.

**Next round:** With larger hook, sc in blo to center back where marker is. Work 2 sc in next st. Sc into blo of remaining sts in round.

Repeat previous round 2 (3, 4, 4, 5) times. Total 24 (32, 40, 40, 50) sc.

## Leg

Continue working 1 sc into blo of each st until sock leg is desired length. Fasten off.

With larger hook, join color B at center back with sl st. Ch 1. Work 1 sc in both loops all around. Join to ch with sl st. Fasten off.

## Heel

**Round 1:** With larger hook and color B, join yarn at point where ch began. Sc 24 (32, 40, 40, 50) sts evenly around heel opening (in both loops). Place marker at end of round.

**Round 2:** Sc 2 tog, [sc 9 (13, 17, 17, 22) sts, sc 3 tog] twice. 20 (28, 36, 36, 46) sts remain.

**Round 3:** [Sc 7 (11, 15, 15, 20) sts, sc 3 tog] twice. 16 (24, 32, 32, 42) sts remain.

Continue in this manner until 16 sts remain.

**Next round:** Sc 2 tog 8 times.

Cut yarn, leaving 8-inch tail. With a tapestry needle, draw tail through blo of remaining sts, drawing them into a tight circle. Fasten off securely.

**Finishing:** Weave in ends. Turn sock so smooth side is on the inside.

**1.** Leaving about a 6-inch tail, form yarn into a ring like you are making a slip knot. Insert the hook into the ring. Do not pull closed; you will work sc into the ring.

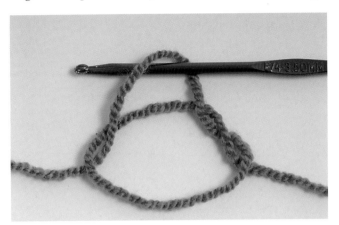

**2.** Work the first round into the ring.

**3.** When the round is complete, gently pull the non-working end of the yarn to tighten the ring.

The hole will disappear almost completely.

**4.** Close ring by joining with a sl st to first st.

**5.** Continue in spiral fashion without joining at the end of each round.

Sassy Socks

An "afterthought" heel is simply a heel that is added after the foot and leg of the sock are completed. The opening for the sock is created after the foot is completed.

**Tip:** Changing hook sizes allows you to create shaping without changing the number of stitches. Follow the pattern instructions for when to use the smaller hook.

**1.** When foot part of sock is desired length, make the number of ch specified in the pattern.

**2.** Count so you skip the same number of sc as the number of ch you just made. This should be exactly halfway around the opening.

**3.** Work a sc into the blo of the stitch you counted to.

**4.** Continue around. When you get back to where the ch starts, work 1 sc into each ch.

**5.** Mark the center back of the ankle, either with a stitch marker or a piece of contrasting yarn. This will show you where to work a decrease on the next round to shape the ankle.

**6.** To work 2 sc tog (decrease), insert hook into next stitch. Yo and pull to front but do not complete the stitch. Insert hook into the next stitch, yo and pull to front.

**7.** To complete the decrease, yo and pull through all 3 loops.

**8.** Continue in pattern, decreasing and then increasing to create a gentle indentation on the back of the ankle.

Sassy Socks

Working 2 or 3 stitches together as indicated creates a nice round shape for the heel.

**1.** Join contrasting color yarn with a sl st at the place where you made the ch for the heel placement.

**2.** Sc in both loops of the stitches around the heel opening.

**3.** On subsequent rounds, work into the back loop only.

**4.** Follow pattern instructions for decreasing on both sides of the heel. At end of pattern, cut yarn, leaving an 8-inch tail. Thread a tapestry needle and pick up the back loops of the remaining stitches.

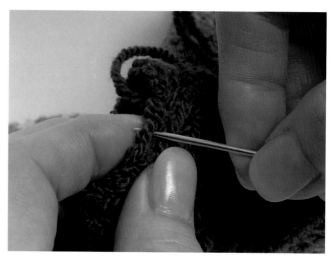

**5.** Pull yarn, drawing stitches into a tight circle. Tie off.

# 7
# Girl's Jumper

Every little girl should have a jumper like this one. It's fancy enough for special occasions, comfortable enough for playtime. The ripple stitch pattern adds texture and interest. A crocheted belt goes through an openwork band that matches the hem trim.

**Finished size:** Sizes 4, 6, 8, 10
(chest 23, 25, 26$^1/_2$, 28 inches)

## Materials:

TLC Cotton Plus Worsted (51 percent
cotton/49 percent acrylic, 3 ounces/85
grams, 155 yards/140 meters)

Color A, 3324 thistle: 5 skeins for sizes
4 and 6, 6 skeins for sizes 8 and 10

Color B, 3643 kiwi: 1 skein (all sizes)

Hook: F/3.75 mm or size needed to
obtain gauge

## Gauge:

Stitches: 8 ripple stitch groups/6 inches;
3 ripple stitch rows/2 inches. Work a
swatch in the pattern, steam block, and
then check your gauge. Adjust hook size
if necessary.

## Stitches and abbreviations:

Chain stitch (ch)

Double crochet (dc)

Single crochet (sc)

Skip (sk)

Slip stitch (sl st)

Stitch (st)

Yo (yarn over)

## To Work a Ripple Stitch Pattern

Ch a multiple of 3 sts + 1 (add 2 for foundation ch).

**Row 1:** 2 dc in third ch from hook. *Skip 2 ch, [1 sc and 2 dc] in next ch, repeat from * to last 3 ch, sk 2 ch, 1 sc in last ch.

**Row 2:** Turn. Ch 2 (this counts as 1 sc), work 2 dc in first sc, * skip 2 dc, [1 sc, 2 dc] in next sc, repeat from *, ending sk 2 dc, 1 sc in second of 2 ch, turn.

Repeat row 2 to continue in pattern.

**Tip:** In the instructions, the number of stitches or rows is for size 4. The number for the larger sizes is given in parentheses. For example:

Work a total of 24 (26, 28, 30) ripple stitch groups

means to work 24 groups for size 4, 26 groups for size 6, 28 groups for size 8, and 30 groups for size 10. Before you start making the jumper, go through the pattern and circle in pencil the numbers for your desired size. This will help you avoid mixing sizes accidentally by reading the wrong number.

## Back and Front
## (they are the same: make 2)

With color A, ch 75 (81, 87, 93).

**Row 1:** 2 dc in third ch from hook. * Skip 2 ch, [1 sc and 2 dc] in next ch, repeat from * to last 3 ch, sk 2 ch, 1 sc in last ch. 24 (26, 28, 30) ripples made.

**Row 2:** Turn. Ch 2 (this counts as 1 sc), work 2 dc in first sc, * skip 2 dc, [1 sc, 2 dc] in next sc, repeat from *, ending sk 2 dc, 1 sc in second of 2 ch, turn.

**Rows 3–10 (3–11, 3–12, 3–13):** Repeat row 2.

**Row 11 (12, 13, 14) (decrease row):** Ch 2. Sk first sc and next 2 dc.

1 sc, 2 sc in next sc. * Sk 2 dc, [1 sc, 2dc] in next sc, repeat from *, ending sk 2 sc, work 1 sc in second of 2 ch.

**Rows 12–18 (13–19, 14–21, 15–23):** Repeat row 2.

**Row 19 (20, 22, 24):** Repeat row 11 (12, 13, 14).

**Rows 20–26 (21–27, 23–29, 25–32):** Repeat row 2.

**Row 27 (28, 30, 33):** Repeat row 11 (12, 13, 14).

**Rows 28–32 (29–33, 31–35, 34–38):** Repeat row 2.

**Row 33 (34, 36, 39):** Repeat row 11(12, 13, 14).

**Rows 34–36 (35–37, 37–39, 40–42):** Repeat row 2.

**Row 37 (38, 40, 43) (openwork row for the belt):** Ch 5. Turn. Sk sc and 2 dc. Dc in next sc.

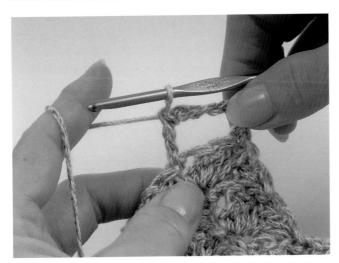

*Ch 2, sk 2 dc, work dc in sc. Repeat from * to last pattern repeat. Sk 2 dc, ch 2, dc in last sc.

**Rows 38–41 (39–43, 41–45, 44–49):** Resume ripple stitch pattern, working in ch sp for the first row.

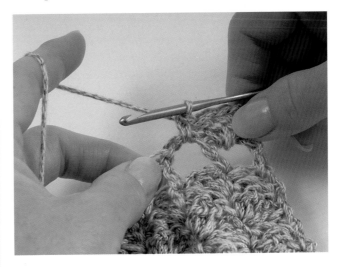

Fasten off.

## Shape Armholes

**Row 1:** Skip 2 ripple stitch groups. Attach yarn with sl st in sp between groups 2 and 3. Work in ripple stitch pattern, leaving last 2 ripples unworked.

**Row 2 (sizes 6, 8, and 10 only):** Work ripple stitch pattern across.

## Straps

**Rows 1–4 (1–5, 1–6, 1–7) (first strap):** Work 2 (2, 3, 3) ripple stitch groups back and forth. Fasten off.

**Tip:** The straps are worked one at a time. Yarn has to be reattached before starting second strap.

**Rows 1–4 (1–5, 1–6, 1–7) (second strap):** With the finished work oriented so you will be working the same direction as you did on the first row of the first strap, attach yarn with a sl st. When you do the same number of ripple stitch patterns as you did on the first step, the attachment point should be where you will come out to the edge of the armhole. (If the work is oriented so you will attach at the outer edge of the armhole, simply do the recommended number of ripple stitch groups, and then turn and continue.) Work 2 (2, 3, 3) ripple stitch groups back and forth. Fasten off.

## Belt

With color B, make a length of moderately loose ch approximately 55 (57, 59, 60) inches long.

**Tip:** If your ch is much tighter or looser than your next row of stitches, the belt will look uneven.

**Row 1:** Starting with second ch from hook, work 1 sc into each ch. Fasten off.

Assemble and trim the jumper following instructions in Skill Workshop.

**1.** Make foundation ch. The ripple st will start in the third ch from the hook.

**2.** Work 2 dc into that ch. Skip 2 ch to find where to work the next ripple.

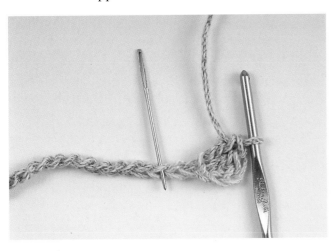

**3.** Work 1 sc and 2 dc into that ch. Continue skipping 2 ch, then working 1 sc and 2 dc into the next ch as you go across.

**4.** For second row, turn. Ch 2 (this counts as 1 sc), work 2 dc in first sc.

**5.** Skip 2 dc and then work 1 sc and 2 dc into the next sc.

**6.** Continue across, ending by skipping the last 2 dc and working 1 sc in the second of the 2 ch.

Girl's Jumper

**1.** Put right sides of front and back together. Using color A and a tapestry needle, sew side seams and top of straps. Do not sew armholes closed!

**2.** Turn right side out. For neckline trim, join color B in any corner around neck. Ch 1. Work sc evenly around front and back of neck, joining with a sl st to the ch to complete the round. Do the same around the armholes.

**3.** The trim around the bottom is worked in little windows like the jumper's waist, where the belt goes. This is done by working 1 round of sc and then making the openwork with ch and dc stitches. Start by attaching color B in any st along the bottom.

**4.** Ch 1. Work sc evenly all around.

**5.** To complete the round, join with a sl st to ch. To start the openwork, ch 6, sk 2 sc, work 1 dc in next sc.

**6.** Ch 2, sk 2, dc in next st all around.

**7.** To complete the trim, join with a sl st to the third ch you made to start the round. Fasten off.

**8.** Thread the belt in and out of the openwork waist.

**9.** Knot the ends of the belt about an inch from each end. Tie in a bow.

# 8

# Felted Handbag

Felting turns wool into matted fabric by wetting, softening, and agitating the fibers so the outer scales, or cuticles, grab onto each other. The technique—accomplished quite easily in the washing machine—works beautifully for handbags. Because the felted material shrinks the stitches and mats them together, there is no need for a lining. This festive handbag intersperses colorful novelty yarn with solid color wool and is topped off with a set of prefabricated handles.

**Finished size (after felting):** Width 8 inches, height 7 inches, not counting handles

**Materials:**

Plymouth Galway (100 percent wool, 100 grams/3.5 ounces, 200 yards/183 meters)

2 skeins color 9 black

Lion Brand Yarn Fancy Fur (polyamide/polyester, 50 grams/1.8 ounces, 35 yards/132 meters)

1 ball color 253, Bold Black

Aunt Lydia's Crochet Thread (100 percent cotton, 150 yards/137 meters)

1 ball color 0012 black

**Tip:** The cotton thread is for sewing the handles onto the bag. If you already have sturdy black thread (about 4 yards), do not buy additional thread.

Hook: Size K

Stitch markers (2)

Handbag handles: 1 pair of handles, 6 inches bottom width from one end to the other, $4^1/2$ inches high, or any handles that fit the bag.

Tapestry needle

**Gauge:**

Gauge is not important for this project. The instructions explain how to get the right size bag after felting.

**Stitches and abbreviations:**

Chain stitch (ch)

Half double crochet (hdc)

Skip (sk)

Slip stitch (sl st)

Stitch (st)

Yo (yarn over)

**Notes:** The handbag is made from the bottom up. A flat oval is created by increasing the number of stitches on each end for several rounds. This makes the base. Once the bag reaches the desired width, the number of stitches remains constant so the sides build up. Working in oval fashion eliminates the need to sew side seams.

Half double stitches work well in felted projects. Single crochet is dense even before felting; when felted, single crochet pieces can be stiff and thick. Double crochet can be used successfully, but the taller stitches may require several trips through the washer to close all of the gaps.

The process of felting shrinks the wool substantially, as anyone who has inadvertently felted a sweater knows! Therefore, the size of the item before felting has to be anywhere from $1^1/4$ to $1^1/2$ times bigger than the finished product. To get a finished width of 8 inches, your prefelted bag needs to be approximately 12 inches wide.

# Felted Handbag

With main color (black), ch 36.

**Round 1:** Hdc in top loop of third ch from hook. This counts as the second hdc, since the 2 other ch count as the first hdc.

**Tip:** Work in top loop only of the foundation ch, since you will be working in the bottom part of the stitch when you come around the bottom of the oval.

Continue to work hdc in each ch until you get to the end, at the first ch you made. Work 3 hdc in this ch. Place stitch marker in the second of those 3 stitches to identify one end of the oval.

Work 1 hdc in the bottom of each ch. Join with sl st to top of ch to finish the oval. Place a stitch marker in that slip stitch.

**Tip:** Make sure there are the same number of stitches between the markers on the top of the oval and the bottom of the oval. You will increase the size of the oval by working 3 hdc in each of those end stitches in subsequent rounds.

**Round 2:** Ch 2. This counts as the first hdc. Work 1 hdc at the base of those ch. Work 1 hdc in each hdc of the previous round until you reach marker. Work 3 hdc into stitch with marker. Move marker to the second of 3 stitches you just made.

Continue around, working 1 hdc in each st. Work 1 hdc at base of ch.

Join with sl st to top of ch to finish the oval.

Sl st into the next st to get to the end. Mark the sl st.

Count to make sure your markers are correctly placed on the ends.

**Rounds 3–4:** Repeat round 2.

If necessary, repeat round 2 until your oval is the desired width (approximately 12 inches). If the oval curls up a little, which is normal, flatten it to measure.

**Round 5:** Now you will stop increasing, so the sides of the bag will start to form. Ch 2. Place stitch marker in the top of the ch so you know where to join when you finish the round. Do not work into the base of the turning ch. Work 1 hdc in each st around. Join with sl st. Sl st into the next stitch to get you to the very end of the oval.

**Tip:** If you need to put your crocheting aside, don't put it down when you have just completed a round. You might start going the wrong direction when you resume. Either leave a few stitches unworked, or work a few stitches on the next round so you know which way you are going.

**Rounds 6–16:** Repeat round 5. Your bag should be approximately 6 inches tall. Fasten off.

**Round 17:** Join novelty yarn with a sl st where you just fastened off. Ch 1. Work 1 sc into each hdc around. Join with sl st.

**Round 18:** Ch 1. Work 1 sc into each sc around. Join with sl st. Fasten off.

**Tip:** If you have not worked with novelty yarn before, it can be hard to find where the stitches are. It helps to look from above. You will see the V shape at the top of each stitch. Feeling with your fingers can also help you figure out exactly where the next stitch is. Count the stitches on each round to make sure you are working the right number.

**Round 19:** Join main color with a sl st where you just fastened off. Ch 2. Work 1 hdc into each sc around. Join with a sl st.

**Round 20:** Ch 2. Work 1 hdc into each hdc around. Join with a sl st.

**Rounds 21–26:** Repeat round 20. Fasten off.

**Round 27:** Repeat round 17.

**Rounds 28–29:** Repeat round 18. Fasten off.

Follow Skill Workshop instructions for felting and attaching handles.

## SKILL WORKSHOP: FELTING

When a woolen item is wet, softened, and agitated, the outermost parts of the fibers begin to grip onto each other. A matted fabric is formed. Individual stitches become almost invisible as the fabric solidifies.

**Note:** You *must* use wool, or a blend with a substantial wool content, for felting. Acrylics and wool substitutes are designed NOT to shrink, making them unsuitable for felting.

If you experiment with other wool yarns, choose ones that do not have a lot of fuzz. Yarns that shed can clog the washing machine and rub off on your clothing. It is a good idea to make a small swatch with your yarn and felt it before embarking on a full-size project.

Felting is accomplished in the washing machine. It can be done multiple times on the same item to shrink it and tighten it even more.

Sometimes shrinkage occurs more in one direction (for example, horizontally) than the other. The surprise of seeing exactly what an item looks like when it comes out of the washer is half the fun!

**1.** Set washing machine to a hot wash and a cold rinse.

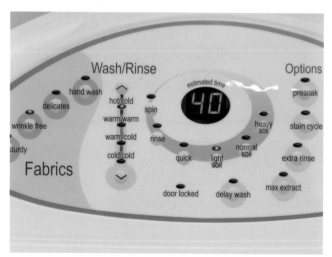

**2.** Put handbag (without handles) in washer. To protect the bag and the washer, you can insert the item into a zippered lingerie bag or pillowcase. You may include the handbag in a full load of wash so you do not waste water.

**3.** Remove handbag from washer when cycle is finished. It will look wet and a little bedraggled and may have a "wet wool" smell. All of these characteristics will disappear as the bag dries.

**4.** Place bag on a clean, lintless towel. If necessary, stuff some clean rags into the bag to help it keep its shape as it dries.

**5.** Now comes the hard part: waiting. Let the bag air-dry completely. Do not put it in the clothes dryer. Do not use the hair dryer. Just be patient. Turn the handbag over periodically so both sides dry.

**Tip:** If you want the stitches to be tighter, repeat the felting process. You do not have to wait for the bag to dry (although you can refelt at that point, also).

Here is an example of what a crocheted swatch looks like before felting, after felting once, and after felting twice.

This is what the crocheted bag looks like before and after felting.

**After**

**Before**

# SKILL WORKSHOP: ATTACHING HANDLES

**1.** Decide which side looks better to you. This will be the outside of the bag. Then, turn it inside out. You will attach the handles so that the attachment points will be on the inside of the finished bag.

**2.** Measure the bag. Position 1 handle so it is centered left to right, a few rows from the top.

**3.** Thread a tapestry needle with crochet thread. To do so, fold the thread in half. Feed the folded end through the eye of the needle. Using folded thread like this will eliminate the need for an initial knot. (Thread will be doubled.)

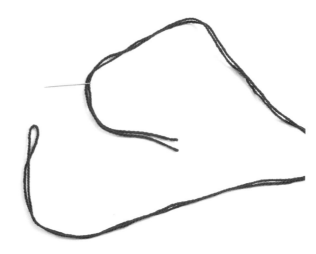

**4.** Push the needle through the bag and the handle connection.

**5.** Pass the thread through the initial loop to catch and hold it in place.

**6.** Pull so the thread is snug.

**7.** Continue sewing until handle is firm. Knot the thread, slide the needle through several stitches of the crochet thread, and cut. Repeat the process with the other end of the handle and with the second handle.

**8.** Turn handbag right side out.

# 9

# Motif Cardigan

This lacy sweater adds drama to anything from jeans to a little black dress. It is worked in soft cotton/acrylic yarn, with the motifs added as you go along, rather than joined at the end. Luxurious edging and a shawl collar finish the sweater beautifully.

If you have been reluctant to attempt motifs because they look so intricate, give this sweater a try. Step-by-step instructions break the process down so that anyone with basic crochet skills can execute the design successfully.

**Finished Size:** Finished bust measurement: S (36 inches), M (42 inches), L (48 inches). Size is altered by the number of motifs made.

## Materials:

Plymouth Yarn Wildflower D.K. (51 percent cotton/49 percent acrylic, 50 grams/1.8 ounces, 137 yards/125 meters)

Color #42: 15 balls for size S, 18 balls for M, 21 balls for L

Hook: G/4 mm or size needed to obtain gauge

Small nonrusting safety pins (approximately 60)

Tapestry needle

## Gauge:

Blocked motif = 6 inches square. Make 1 complete motif, steam block, and measure it before you continue. Switch to a different size hook if your gauge is off.

## Stitches and abbreviations:

Back loop only (blo)

Chain stitch (ch)

Double crochet (dc)

Half double crochet (hdc)

Reverse single crochet (rsc)

Single crochet (sc)

Skip (sk)

Slip stitch (sl st)

Space (sp)

Stitch (st)

Triple treble crochet (trtr)

V-stitch

Yo (yarn over)

To work a reverse single crochet, insert the hook in the specified stitch to the right. Yo, pull to front. Yo, pull through both loops. The only difference between the rsc and a regular sc is that it moves from left to right.

To work a triple treble, wrap yarn around hook 4 times. Insert hook into the work. Yo and pull through to front. (Yo and pull through 2 loops) 5 times.

To make a V-stitch, work a dc, ch 1, dc in the same space.

All sizes should make motifs 1 through 16 for first sleeve and motifs 17 through 32 for second sleeve. In addition:

Size S, make motifs 33 through 52

Size M, make motifs 53 through 75

Size L, make motifs 76 through 104

**Tip:** To make assembly easier, pin a small piece of paper with the motif's number onto each motif as soon as you complete it. This will help clarify where to attach subsequent squares and where to join the sleeves to the body. Follow the chart to position the motifs properly.

## Motif 1

Ch 6. Sl st into first ch to make ring.

**Round 1:** Ch 1, (sc in ring, ch 12) 11 times . . .

. . . sc in ring, ch 6, trtr in ring.

This makes 12 petals. The trtr brings the twelfth petal up to the same height as the other petals.

**Tip:** Make sure the ring does not flip over while you are working the petals into it. You should always be moving around the circle in the same direction. Do not twist the petals as you make the ch.

**Round 2:** Ch 1, sl st into center of the same petal. Ch 4 (counts as dc and ch 1) . . .

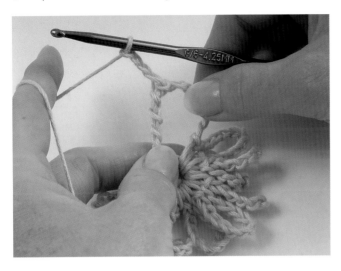

. . . dc in same sp . . .

. . . *ch 4, (dc, ch 1, dc) in next ch 12 spaces *.

Repeat from * to * 10 more times, ch 4, sl stitch into third ch from beginning of round to join.

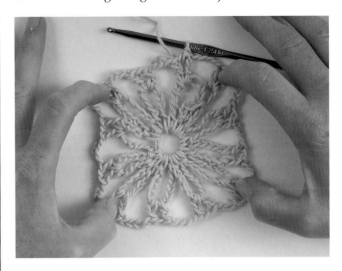

**Round 3:** Sl st into first ch 1 sp, ch 4 (counts as dc and ch 1), dc into same sp, *ch 5, (dc, ch 1, dc) in next ch 1 sp.*

Repeat from * to * 10 more times. Ch 5, sl st into third ch from beginning of round.

**Tip:** Notice that as the motif expands, there are more chains between each segment. On round 2, there are 4 chains. On round 3, there are 5 chains. If you guessed that there will be 6 chains on round 4, you're right.

**Round 4:** Sl st into first ch 1 sp, ch 4 (counts as dc and ch 1), dc in same sp, *ch 6, (dc, ch 1, dc) in next ch 1 sp *.

Repeat from * to * 10 more times. Ch 6, sl st into third ch from beginning of round. Fasten off.

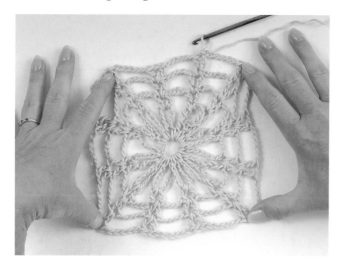

**Tip:** Look how everything flows out from the middle through the chain petals through the V-stitches. The V-stitches (dc, ch 1, dc) are all lined up.

Follow the diagrams to make and assemble the motifs. You will make one sleeve by joining new motifs to completed ones, and then make the other sleeve. The underarm seams are sewn to form the sleeves into their tube shapes. Next you will make the body, and then sew the sleeves on the sweater. Finally, you will add trim around the cuffs, neckline, front, and bottom.

Remember, all sizes make motifs 1 through 16 for the first sleeve and 17 through 32 for the second sleeve. In addition:

Size S, make motifs 33 through 52
Size M, make motifs 53 through 75
Size L, make motifs 76 through 104

Joining motifs as you go along eliminates the need to sew them together after you have created them separately. Once you understand the logic behind the joins, the method will come easily.

Here's how it works for a 1-sided join, like with motifs 1 and 2 on the sleeve. Each complete motif square consists of 4 rounds. When you join 2 motifs, the first one (in this case, #1, which we will call the "completed motif") will already be a finished square of 4 complete rounds. As you work the outermost round (round 4) of the current motif, #2, you will join the motif in progress to the completed motif at 4 points by working a sl st into the 4 corresponding ch 1 spaces in the finished square. Then you will continue around the rest of the current motif to finish its fourth round.

**1.** Crochet the next motif (#2) through the first 3 rounds, like for any other motif. Start round 4 just like before, sl st into first ch 1 sp, ch 4 (counts as dc and ch 1), dc in same sp, ch 6.

**2.** This is where you will work into the current square and the completed square. First, work 1 dc and ch 1 into the next ch sp on the current square. Then find the corresponding ch sp on the completed square. Work a sl st into that space to attach the motifs.

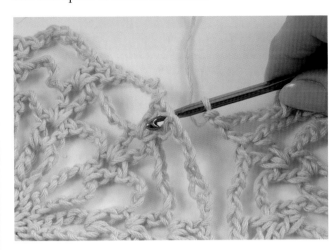

**Tip:** Only the sl st is worked into the completed motif. All other stitches are worked on the current motif.

**3.** Now you will go back to working on the current square. Ch 1, dc in the same ch sp where you made the dc before the join.

Motif Cardigan

The motifs are joined in 1 spot.

The motif on the right (the current motif) is smaller because the outermost round is not yet complete.

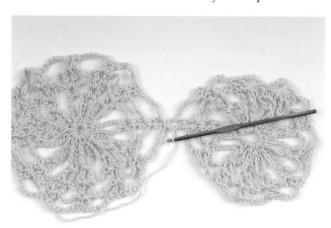

**4.** Ch 6. Work 1 dc into next ch sp of current motif. Ch 1. Sl st into adjacent ch sp on completed square to join. Ch 1, work 1 dc into same ch sp of current motif where you already worked 1 dc.

**Tip:** Make sure you are using the adjacent ch sp from the completed square. Do not skip any ch sp, or the squares will not line up and you will have to rip out the joins and start over.

**5.** Repeat the process a third time. Here is what it looks like when the motifs are joined in 3 places.

**6.** Repeat 1 more time so the motifs are joined in 4 places.

**7.** Now continue working round 4 on the current motif. No more joins are necessary. When you get back to the beginning after the final ch 6, sl st into third ch from the beginning of the round. Fasten off.

Joining 1 motif on 2 sides is accomplished in a similar fashion. For example, motif 6 attaches to 2 other motifs: 5 and 3. Start by joining motif 6 to 5. When you get to the fourth connection between the 2 motifs, work the sl st into the same ch sp where motifs 5 and 4 are connected. This connection counts as the fourth one between motifs 6 and 5, and the first one between motifs 6 and 3. Work 3 more connections and then complete the motif.

**Tip:** When connecting a motif in a corner where 2 motifs have already been joined, work the sl st into the same space that was used to connect the first 2. This keeps the connections neat and firm.

Work the motifs in number order, joining as indicated in the chart. Remember to pin a piece of paper with the number of the motif on each finished square as you go along. Joining instructions are given for the motif in progress. (See Skill Workshop.)

| Sleeve 1 (all sizes) | | | |
|---|---|---|---|
| 1 | 2 | 3 | 4 |
| 8 | 7 | 6 | 5 |
| 9 | 10 | 11 | 12 |
| 16 | 15 | 14 | 13 |

For sleeve 1, motifs 1-8-9-16 are the shoulder end, and 4-5-12-13 are the cuff end. Sew the underarm seam as follows (with the right sides of motifs together so sleeve is inside out): 1 to 16, 2 to 15, 3 to 14, 4 to 13.

| Sleeve 2 (all sizes) | | | |
|---|---|---|---|
| 17 | 18 | 19 | 20 |
| 24 | 23 | 22 | 21 |
| 25 | 26 | 27 | 28 |
| 32 | 31 | 30 | 29 |

For sleeve 2, motifs 17-24-25-32 are the shoulder end, and 20-21-28-29 are the cuff end. Sew the underarm seam as follows (with the right sides of motifs together so sleeve is inside out): 17 to 32, 18 to 31, 19 to 30, 20 to 29.

Now make the motifs for the body. Work the motifs in number order, joining as indicated in the chart and text below. The numbers here start at the hem and work their way up.

| Body (size S) | | | | | |
|---|---|---|---|---|---|
| | | | 52 | | |
| | | | ▽51 | | |
| 45 | 46 | 47 | 48 | 49 | 50 |
| 44 | 43 | 42 | 41 | 40 | 39 |
| 33 | 34 | 35 | 36 | 37 | 38 |

| Body (size M) | | | | | | |
|---|---|---|---|---|---|---|
| | | | 75 | | | |
| | | | ▽74 | | | |
| 67 | 68 | 69 | 70 | 71 | 72 | 73 |
| 66 | 65 | 64 | 63 | 62 | 61 | 60 |
| 53 | 54 | 55 | 56 | 57 | 58 | 59 |

| Body (size L) | | | | | | | |
|---|---|---|---|---|---|---|---|
| | | | 104 | 105 | | | |
| ▽103 | | | 102 | 101 | | | ▽100 |
| 92 | 93 | 94 | 95 | 96 | 97 | 98 | 99 |
| 91 | 90 | 89 | 88 | 87 | 86 | 85 | 84 |
| 76 | 77 | 78 | 79 | 80 | 81 | 82 | 83 |

This is motif 51 for size S; 74 for M; 100 and 103 for L

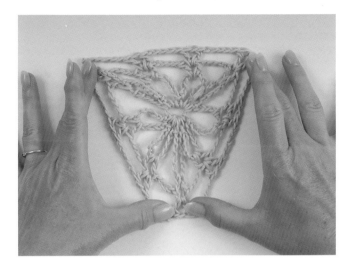

**Tip:** The triangular motif is worked like the square motifs, except it has 9 petals instead of 12.

Ch 5. Sl st into first ch to make ring.

**Round 1:** Ch 1, (sc in ring, ch 12) 8 times, sc in ring, ch 6, trtr in ring.

**Round 2:** Ch 1, sl st into same sp, ch 4 (counts as dc and ch 1), dc in same sp, *ch 4, (dc, ch 1, dc) in next ch 12 spaces *. Repeat from * to * 8 more times. Ch 4, sl st into third ch from beginning of round.

**Round 3:** Sl st into first ch 1 sp, ch 4 (counts as dc and ch 1), dc into same sp, * ch 5, (dc, ch 1, dc) in next ch 1 sp *. Repeat from * to * 8 more times. Ch 5, sl st into third ch from beginning of round.

**Round 4:** Sl st into first ch 1 sp, ch 4 (counts as dc and ch 1), dc in same sp, *ch 6, dc in next ch sp, ch 1, sl st into corresponding ch sp on the completed motif, ch 1, dc back in motif you are currently making where you already worked 1 dc. Repeat from * 3 more times so that the motifs are joined in 4 places.

**Tip:** The fourth join is at the bottom point of the triangular motif.

Continue working round 4, joining to the next motif. After that, no more joins are necessary. Complete the third side, across the top of the triangle. When you are all the way to the beginning after the final ch 6, sl st into third ch from the beginning of the round. Fasten off.

Make sure sleeves are inside out. You will sew them to the wrong side of the sweater body so the seams do not show. Pin the sleeves in place before sewing them—the sleeves and body flow together, and it is much easier to see how everything fits if you pin it first.

For the small size, join the first sleeve to the body by sewing motif 1 to 50; 16 to 48 and 51; 9 to 52. Join the second sleeve to the body by sewing motif 17 to 47 and 51; 24 to 52; 32 to 45.

For the medium size, join the first sleeve to the body by sewing motif 16 to 67; 1 to 69 and 74; 8 to 75. Join the second sleeve to the body by sewing motif 17 to 73; 32 to 71 and 74; 25 to 75.

For the large size, join the first sleeve to the body by sewing motif 16 to 93 and 103; 1 to 94 and 102; 8 to 104. Join the second sleeve to the body by sewing motif 17 to 98 and 100; 32 to 97 and 101; 25 to 105.

**Tip:** Position the completed part of your work to take on the shape of the finished garment, either by arranging it on a hanger or by draping it on a willing friend. This will help you visualize where the sleeves attach to the body. Seeing the shape emerge in 3 dimensions is very helpful. Use safety pins to hold things in place before you sew the sleeves to the body.

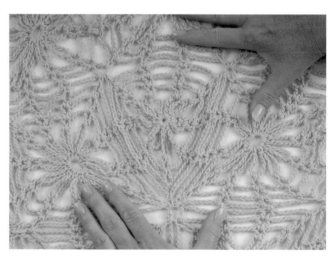

*Motif Cardigan*

## Cuffs

**Round 1:** With right side facing, join with sl st to any dc at edge of sleeve. Ch 1, * sc in dc, sc in ch 1 sp, sc in dc, 6 sc in ch 6 sp *. Repeat from * to * around. Join with sl st to first sc.

**Rounds 2–5:** Repeat round 1.

**Round 6:** Ch 1, reverse single crochet (rsc) into first sc, sk 1, ch 2. (Rsc, sk 1, ch 2) around, ending with a sl st to join. Fasten off.

Repeat for second sleeve.

## Edging

The edging is worked in 3 parts. First, edging is worked all around the sweater. Next, the collar is created. Last, edging is worked around the border and the collar to integrate the collar and trim.

### FIRST PART OF EDGING
**Round 1:** With right side facing, join with sl st to any dc along perimeter of sweater. Ch 1, sc in same st, sc in ch 1 sp, sc in next dc, 6 sc in next ch 6 space. Continue working sc around in this manner, except work 2 sc, ch 2, 2 sc into corner V-stitch at lower edge of body (motifs 33 and 38 for S, motifs 53 and 59 for M, motifs 76 and 83 for L).

**Rounds 2–5:** Repeat round 1. Fasten off.

### COLLAR
**Row 1:** With right side facing, join with sl stitch along front of edge of motif 50 (73, 100). Ch 2. Hdc in back loop only (blo) in each sc across to edge of motif 45 (67, 103) exactly opposite where you started. Turn.

**Rows 2–4:** Ch 2, hdc blo in each st across.

**Row 5:** Sl st into first 4 st, ch 2, hdc blo into each st across, skipping last 3 st. Turn.

**Row 6:** Repeat row 5: Fasten off.

### LAST PART OF EDGING
**Round 1:** With right side facing, join with sl st to any st along perimeter of sweater. Ch 1, sc into each st around, putting 3 sc into each corner ch 2 sp.

**Round 2:** Ch 1, sc into each st around, putting 3 sc into center st of each corner.

**Rounds 3–5:** Repeat round 2.

**Round 6:** (Rsc, ch 2, sk 1 st) around (moving left to right to execute reverse single crochet). Sl st into first st to join. Fasten off.

## Belt (optional)

Ch 256.

**Row 1:** Starting with second ch from hook, work 1 sc in top loop of each ch.

**Rows 2–4:** Ch 1. Turn. Work 1 sc into each sc across. Fasten off.

**Row 5:** Turn work around. You will work into the remaining loop of the initial ch. Join yarn into first ch with sl st. Ch 1. Work 1 sc into remaining loops of each ch across.

**Rows 6–8:** Ch 1. Turn. Work 1 sc into each sc across. Do not fasten off.

**Border:** Do not turn. Ch 1. Work (1 rsc, sk 1, ch 2) around. Join with sl st to ch. Fasten off.

# Appendices

## Standard Body Measurements/Sizing

Most crochet and knitting pattern instructions will provide general sizing information, such as the chest or bust measurements of a completed garment. Many patterns also include detailed schematics or line drawings. These drawings show specific garment measurements (bust/chest, neckline, back, waist, sleeve length, etc.) in all the different pattern sizes. To insure proper fit, always review all of the sizing information provided in a pattern before you begin.

Following are several sizing charts. These charts show Chest, Center Back Neck-to-Cuff, Back Waist Length, Cross Back, and Sleeve Length **actual body measurements** for babies, children, women, and men. These measurements are given in both inches and centimeters.

When sizing sweaters, the fit is based on actual chest/bust measurements, plus ease (additional inches or centimeters). The first chart entitled "Fit" recommends the amount of ease to add to body measurements if you prefer a close-fitting garment, an oversized garment, or something in-between.

The next charts provide average lengths for children's, women's and men's garments.

Both the Fit and Length charts are simply guidelines. For individual body differences, changes can be made in body and sleeve lengths when appropriate. However, consideration must be given to the project pattern. Certain sizing changes may alter the appearance of a garment.

### HOW TO MEASURE

**1. Chest/Bust**
Measure around the fullest part of the chest/bust. Do not draw the tape too tightly.

**2. Center Back Neck-to-Cuff**
With arm slightly bent, measure from back base of neck across shoulder around bend of elbow to wrist.

**3. Back Waist Length**
Measure from the most prominent bone at base of neck to the natural waistline.

**4. Cross Back**
Measure from shoulder to shoulder.

**5. Sleeve Length**
With arm slightly bent, measure from armpit to cuff.

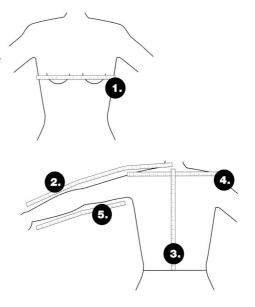

### FIT

**Very-close fitting:** Actual chest/bust measurement or less
**Close-fitting:** 1–2"/2.5–5cm
**Standard-fitting:** 2–4"/5–10cm
**Loose-fitting:** 4–6"/10–15cm
**Oversized:** 6"/15cm or more

### LENGTH FOR CHILDREN

**Waist length:** Actual body measurement
**Hip length:** 2"/5cm down from waist
**Tunic length:** 6"/15cm down from waist

### LENGTH FOR WOMEN

**Waist length:** Actual body measurement
**Hip length:** 6"/15cm down from waist
**Tunic length:** 11"/28cm down from waist

### LENGTH FOR MEN

Men's length usually varies only 1–2"/ 2.5–5cm from the actual "back hip length" measurement (*see chart*)

| Baby's size | 3 months | 6 months | 12 months | 18 months | 24 months |
|---|---|---|---|---|---|
| **1.** Chest (in.) | 16 | 17 | 18 | 19 | 20 |
| (cm.) | 40.5 | 43 | 45.5 | 48 | 50.5 |
| **2.** Center Back Neck-to-Cuff | 10½ | 11½ | 12½ | 14 | 18 |
| | 26.5 | 29 | 31.5 | 35.5 | 45.5 |
| **3.** Back Waist Length | 6 | 7 | 7½ | 8 | 8½ |
| | 15.5 | 17.5 | 19 | 20.5 | 21.5 |
| **4.** Cross Back (Shoulder to shoulder) | 7¼ | 7¾ | 8¼ | 8½ | 8¾ |
| | 18.5 | 19.5 | 21 | 21.5 | 22 |
| **5.** Sleeve Length to Underarm | 6 | 6½ | 7½ | 8 | 8½ |
| | 15.5 | 16.5 | 19 | 20.5 | 21.5 |

| Child's size | 2 | 4 | 6 | 8 | 10 |
|---|---|---|---|---|---|
| **1.** Chest (in.) | 21 | 23 | 25 | 26½ | 28 |
| (cm.) | 53 | 58.5 | 63.5 | 67 | 71 |
| **2.** Center Back Neck-to-Cuff | 18 | 19½ | 20½ | 22 | 24 |
| | 45.5 | 49.5 | 52 | 56 | 61 |
| **3.** Back Waist Length | 8½ | 9½ | 10½ | 12½ | 14 |
| | 21.5 | 24 | 26.5 | 31.5 | 35.5 |
| **4.** Cross Back (Shoulder to shoulder) | 9¼ | 9¾ | 10¼ | 10¾ | 11¼ |
| | 23.5 | 25 | 26 | 27 | 28.5 |
| **5.** Sleeve Length to Underarm | 8½ | 10½ | 11½ | 12½ | 13½ |
| | 21.5 | 26.5 | 29 | 31.5 | 34.5 |

| Child's (cont.) | 12 | 14 | 16 |
|---|---|---|---|
| **1.** Chest (in.) | 30 | 31½ | 32½ |
| *(cm.)* | *76* | *80* | *82.5* |
| **2.** Center Back Neck-to-Cuff | 26 | 27 | 28 |
| | *66* | *68.5* | *71* |
| **3.** Back Waist Length | 15 | 15½ | 16 |
| | *38* | *39.5* | *40.5* |
| **4.** Cross Back (Shoulder to Shoulder) | 12 | 12¼ | 13 |
| | *30.5* | *31* | *33* |
| **5.** Sleeve Length to Underarm | 15 | 16 | 16½ |
| | *38* | *40.5* | *42* |

| Woman's size | X-Small | Small | Medium | Large |
|---|---|---|---|---|
| **1.** Bust (in.) | 28–30 | 32–34 | 36–38 | 40–42 |
| *(cm.)* | *71–76* | *81–86* | *91.5–96.5* | *101.5–106.5* |
| **2.** Center Back Neck-to-Cuff | 27–27½ | 28–28½ | 29–29½ | 30–30½ |
| | *68.5–70* | *71–72.5* | *73.5–75* | *76–77.5* |
| **3.** Back Waist Length | 16½ | 17 | 17¼ | 17½ |
| | *42* | *43* | *43.5* | *44.5* |
| **4.** Cross Back (Shoulder to Shoulder) | 14–14½ | 14½–15 | 16–16½ | 17–17½ |
| | *35.5–37* | *37–38* | *40.5–42* | *43–44.5* |
| **5.** Sleeve Length to Underarm | 16½ | 17 | 17 | 17½ |
| | *42* | *43* | *43* | *44.5* |

| Woman's (cont.) | 1X | 2X | 3X | 4X | 5X |
|---|---|---|---|---|---|
| **1.** Bust (in.) | 44–46 | 48–50 | 52–54 | 56–58 | 60–62 |
| *(cm.)* | *111.5–117* | *122–127* | *132–137* | *142–147* | *152–158* |
| **2.** Center Back Neck-to-Cuff | 31–31½ | 31½–32 | 32½–33 | 32½–33 | 33–33½ |
| | *78.5–80* | *80–81.5* | *82.5–84* | *82.5–84* | *84–85* |
| **3.** Back Waist Length | 17¾ | 18 | 18 | 18½ | 18½ |
| | *45* | *45.5* | *45.5* | *47* | *47* |
| **4.** Cross Back (Shoulder to Shoulder) | 17½ | 18 | 18 | 18½ | 18½ |
| | *44.5* | *45.5* | *45.5* | *47* | *47* |
| **5.** Sleeve Length to Underarm | 17½ | 18 | 18 | 18½ | 18½ |
| | *44.5* | *45.5* | *45.5* | *47* | *47* |

## Standard Body Measurements/Sizing continued

| Man's Size | Small | Medium | Large | X-Large | XX-Large |
|---|---|---|---|---|---|
| **1.** Chest (in.) | 34–36 | 38–40 | 42–44 | 46–48 | 50–52 |
| (cm.) | 86–91.5 | 96.5–101.5 | 106.5–111.5 | 116.5–122 | 127–132 |
| **2.** Center Back Neck-to-Cuff | 32–32½ | 33–33½ | 34–34½ | 35–35½ | 36–36½ |
| | 81–82.5 | 83.5–85 | 86.5–87.5 | 89–90 | 91.5–92.5 |
| **3.** Back Hip Length | 25–25½ | 26½–26¾ | 27–27¼ | 27½–27¾ | 28–28½ |
| | 63.5–64.5 | 67.5–68 | 68.5–69 | 69.5–70.5 | 71–72.5 |
| **4.** Cross Back (Shoulder to Shoulder) | 15½–16 | 16½–17 | 17½–18 | 18–18½ | 18½–19 |
| | 39.5–40.5 | 42–43 | 44.5–45.5 | 45.5–47 | 47–48 |
| **5.** Sleeve Length to Underarm | 18 | 18½ | 19½ | 20 | 20½ |
| | 45.5 | 47 | 49.5 | 50.5 | 52 |

### Head Circumference Chart

| | Infant/Child | | | | Adult | |
|---|---|---|---|---|---|---|
| | **Premie** | **Baby** | **Toddler** | **Child** | **Woman** | **Man** |
| **6.** Circumference | | | | | | |
| (in.) | 12 | 14 | 16 | 18 | 20 | 22 |
| (cm.) | 30.5 | 35.5 | 40.5 | 45.5 | 50.5 | 56 |

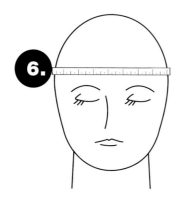

For an accurate head measure, place a tape measure across the forehead and measure around the full circumference of the head. Keep the tape snug for accurate results.

## Standard Yarn Weight System

**Categories of yarn, gauge ranges, and recommended needle and hook sizes**

| Yarn Weight Symbol & Category Names | 1 Super Fine | 2 Fine | 3 Light | 4 Medium | 5 Bulky | 6 Super Bulky |
|---|---|---|---|---|---|---|
| Type of Yarns in Category | Sock, Fingering, Baby | Sport, Baby | DK, Light Worsted | Worsted, Afghan, Aran | Chunky, Craft, Rug | Bulky, Roving |
| Knit Gauge Range* in Stockinette Stitch to 4 inches | 27–32 sts | 23–26 sts | 21–24 sts | 16–20 sts | 12–15 sts | 6–11 sts |
| Recommended Needle in Metric Size Range | 2.25–3.25 mm | 3.25–3.75 mm | 3.75–4.5 mm | 4.5–5.5 mm | 5.5–8 mm | 8 mm and larger |
| Recommended Needle U.S. Size Range | 1 to 3 | 3 to 5 | 5 to 7 | 7 to 9 | 9 to 11 | 11 and larger |
| Crochet Gauge* Ranges in Single Crochet to 4 inch | 21–32 sts | 16–20 sts | 12–17 sts | 11–14 sts | 8–11 sts | 5–9 sts |
| Recommended Hook in Metric Size Range | 2.25–3.5 mm | 3.5–4.5 mm | 4.5–5.5 mm | 5.5–6.5 mm | 6.5–9 mm | 9 mm and larger |
| Recommended Hook U.S. Size Range | B–1 to E–4 | E–4 to 7 | 7 to I–9 | I–9 to K–10½ | K–10½ to M–13 | M–13 and larger |

**\* GUIDELINES ONLY: The above reflect the most commonly used gauges and needle or hook sizes for specific yarn categories.**

# Resources

**BOOKS**

Barnden, Betty. *The Crochet Stitch Bible*. Iola, WI: Krause Publications, 2004.

Chin, Lily M. *Knit and Crochet with Beads*. Loveland, CO: Interweave Press, 2004.

Eckman, Edie. *The Crochet Answer Book*. North Adams, MA: Storey Publishing, 2005.

Matthews, Anne. *Vogue Dictionary of Crochet Stitches*. Newton, UK: David & Charles, 1987.

Reader's Digest. *The Ultimate Sourcebook of Knitting and Crochet Stitches*. Pleasantville, NY: Reader's Digest, 2003.

Silverman, Sharon Hernes. *Basic Crocheting*. Mechanicsburg, PA: Stackpole Books, 2006.

Wiseman, Nancy M. *Crochet with Wire*. Loveland, CO: Interweave Press, 2005.

**DESIGNER WEBSITES**

Sharon Hernes Silverman
*www.sharonsilverman.com*

Annie Modesitt
*www.anniemodesitt.com*

Kristin Omdahl
*www.styledbykristin.com*

**YARN, WIRE, BEADS, AND OTHER SUPPLIES**

Your local yarn shop is the best source for supplies and advice. The staff is knowledgeable about yarns from many different manufacturers and can help you substitute one yarn for another or find just the right color combination. Questions are welcomed and advice is given freely. Check the shop's schedule for specialty classes to add to your skill set, and get on the mailing list so you can find out when yarn is on sale.

Catalogs and online retailers sell yarn and equipment. Hundreds of providers exist; you can find them on the Internet by searching for "yarn," "crocheting," or "free patterns." Here are just a few sources.

A Garden of Yarn
1-888-226-KNIT (5648)
*www.agardenofyarn.com*

Art Yarns
914-428-0333
*www.artyarns.com*

Artistic Wire Ltd.
630-530-7567
*www.artisticwire.com*

Beads World, Inc.
212-302-1199
*www.beadsworldusa.com*

Bernat
888-368-8401
*www.bernat.com*

Berrocco Yarns
508-278-2527
*www.berrocco.com*

Caron
*www.caron.com*

Classic Elite Yarns
800-343-0308
*www.classiceliteyarns.com*

Herrschners
800-441-0838
*www.herrschners.com*

Karabella Yarns
212-684-2665
*www.karabellayarns.com*

Kraemer Yarns
800-759-5601
*www.kraemeryarnshop.com*

Lion Brand Yarn
800-258-9276
*www.lionbrand.com*

Mary Maxim Exclusive Needlework and Crafts
800-962-9504
*www.marymaxim.com*

Patternworks
800-438-5464
*www.patternworks.com*

Plymouth Yarn Company
215-788-0459
*www.plymouthyarn.com*

Yarn Market
888-996-9276
*www.yarnmarket.com*

## OTHER RESOURCES FOR CROCHETERS

Craft Yarn Council of America
The craft yarn industry's trade association has educational links and free projects.
*www.craftyarncouncil.com*

Crochet Guild of America
The national association for crocheters and the publisher of *Crochet!* magazine. The association sponsors conventions, offers correspondence courses, and maintains a membership directory.
*www.crochet.org*

Interweave Press
Although more focused on knitting and other fibers arts than crocheting, Interweave publishes a special issue of their *Interweave Knits* magazine dedicated to crocheting.
*www.interweave.com*

# Stackpole Basics

## All the Skills and Tools You Need to Get Started

- **Straightforward, expert instruction on a variety of crafts, hobbies, and sports**
- **Step-by-step, easy-to-follow format**
- **Current information on equipment and prices for the beginner**
- **Full-color photography and illustrations**
- **Convenient lay-flat spiral binding**

**BASIC STAINED GLASS MAKING**
$19.95, 144 pages, 754 color photos,
24 illustrations, 0-8117-2846-3

**BASIC KNITTING**
$19.95, 108 pages, 377 color photos,
50 color illustrations, 0-8117-3178-2

**BASIC CANDLE MAKING**
$19.95, 104 pages, 600 color photos,
0-8117-2476-X

**BASIC DRIED FLOWER ARRANGING**
$16.95, 96 pages, 234 color photos,
0-8117-2863-3

**BASIC QUILTING**
$19.95, 128 pages, 437 color photos,
11 illustrations, 0-8117-3348-3

**BASIC PICTURE FRAMING**
$19.95, 108 pages, 374 color photos,
0-8117-3109-X

**BASIC JEWELRY MAKING**
$19.95, 116 pages, 490 color photos,
12 illustrations, 0-8117-3263-0

**BASIC CROCHETING**
$19.95, 120 pages, 219 color photos,
27 illustrations, 0-8117-3316-5

Available at your favorite retailer,
or from Stackpole Books at (800) 732-3669

## STACKPOLE BOOKS

www.stackpolebooks.com